Easy World Wide Web
with Netscape

A V I A C O M   S E R V I C E

The Information SuperLibrary™

Bookstore

Search

What's New

Reference Desk

Software Library

Newsletter

Company Overviews

Yellow Pages

Internet Starter Kit

HTML Workshop

Win a Free T-Shirt!

Macmillan Computer Publishing

Site Map

Talk to Us

CHECK OUT THE BOOKS IN THIS LIBRARY.

You'll find thousands of shareware files and over 1600 computer books designed for both technowizards and technophobes. You can browse through 700 sample chapters, get the latest news on the Net, and find just about anything using our massive search directories.

All Macmillan Computer Publishing books are available at your local bookstore.

We're open 24-hours a day, 365 days a year.

You don't need a card.

We don't charge fines.

And you can be as LOUD as you want.

The Information SuperLibrary
http://www.mcp.com/mcp/   ftp.mcp.com

Easy World Wide Web
with Netscape

Jim Minatel

Easy World Wide Web with Netscape

Copyright © 1996 by Que® Corporation

Library of Congress Catalog No.: 95-68632

ISBN: 0-7897-0279-7

98 97 96 95   6 5 4 3 2

Interpretation of the printing code: the rightmost double-digit number is the year of the book's printing; the rightmost single-digit number, the number of the book's printing. For example, a printing code of 95-1 shows that the first printing of the book occurred in 1995.

President: Roland Elgey

Publisher: Stacy Hiquet

Managing Editor: Sandra Doell

Director of Marketing: Lynn E. Zingraf

Credits

Acquisitions Editor
Cheryl D. Willoughby

Production Editor
Mitzi Foster Gianakos

Technical Editors
Alp Berker
Alfonso Hermida

Figure Specialist
Cari Skaggs

Book Designers
Sandra Stevenson-Schroeder
Amy Peppler-Adams

Cover Designer
Dan Armstrong

Acquisitions Coordinator
Ruth Slates

Operations Coordinator
Patty Brooks

Editorial Assistant
Andrea Duvall

Production Team
Claudia Bell
Anne Dickerson
DiMonique Ford
Aren Howell
Daryl Kessler
Elizabeth Lewis
Kaylene Riemen
Kristine Simmons
Michael Thomas
Jody York

Indexer
Carol Sheehan

Composed in *Stone Serif* and *MCPdigital* by Que Corporation

Dedication

To Mom, Dad, and Angie (not necessarily in that order). Thanks for all of the years of support and encouragement.

About the Author

Jim Minatel is a Publishing Manager with Que Publishing in Indianapolis. He specializes in books about the Internet and Multimedia for Windows users. He holds B.A. degrees in Math and Physics from Wabash College and a M.S. in Math from Chicago State University.

Jim has developed several best-selling books including *Special Edition Using the Internet, Second Edition* and *Using the World Wide Web*. He has been a contributing author on several books on Internet topics for Que.

Jim can be reached by e-mail at **jminatel@que.mcp.com**.

Acknowledgments

I owe thanks to the many people at Que who have helped me with this project. First and foremost, thanks to Mitzi for keeping the manuscript clean and turning this around on an unbelievable schedule. Thanks to Cheryl for signing me to write this. Thanks to Brad and Stacy for having the vision to let me write this. And I can't forget Stephanie who picked up the slack on some other key projects to free up some time for me on this. And most of all, thanks to all the people I work with at Que on a daily basis who I also push and never thank.

Trademark Acknowledgments

All terms mentioned in this book that are known to be trademarks or service marks have been appropriately capitalized. Que Corporation cannot attest to the accuracy of this information. Use of a term in this book should not be regarded as affecting the validity of any trademark or service mark.

Contents at a Glance

Contents

Part IV: Bookmarks: Shortcuts to Your Favorite Places 75

Part V: Experiencing Multimedia 103

Part VI: Saving, Opening, and Printing Files 129

Introduction

What You Can Do with Netscape

Netscape Navigator is an application for use with the World Wide Web. Netscape features a very easy-to-use graphical interface complete with many visual tools. Netscape's toolbar with buttons for common tasks and directory bar with buttons for frequently used destinations on the Web give Netscape a true point and click interface.

Here are some specific tasks you can accomplish with Netscape:

■ *Open Web documents, called pages, from sites all over the world.* These pages can contain text about any subject, pictures, sounds, and even movies. This is the main task you will use Netscape for. You will learn how you can jump from one page to another, how to understand and enter the address for a page, and how to change the page that Netscape loads when it first starts. All of these tasks are covered in Part II, "Navigating the Web with Netscape," in this book.

■ *Search for documents on the Web.* Netscape can be used to open Web pages that contain lists of other pages or tools to help you find other pages. Using these tools to search the Web is covered in Part III, "Finding Your Way on the Web."

■ *Create lists of your favorite sites.* Navigating the Web wouldn't be much fun if you didn't have a way to get back to documents that you use often. Netscape helps you by letting you create lists of pages that you use frequently and want to be able to get to easily. These tasks are covered in Part IV, "Bookmarks: Shortcuts to Your Favorite Places."

■ *View multimedia.* With Netscape, you can download and view pictures that you find on the Web. You can also listen to sound files and play movies. Netscape also lets you save these multimedia files for use at a later time with another application. Multimedia on the Web with Netscape is covered in Part V, "Experiencing Multimedia."

■ *Save and print files from the Web.* Although a big advantage of the Web is that you have all of this information at your fingertips without having to have it on your computer, you can save the documents, or even print them, for later reference. Part VI, "Saving, Opening, and Printing Files," covers these topics.

■ *You can read the news with Netscape.* Another part of the Internet separate from the Web is called UseNet news. Although Netscape is made for the Web, it also has features to read UseNet news. The news you read can be about any topic you can imagine. Netscape allows you to read articles posted by others, reply to them, and even post your own articles. UseNet is covered in Part VII, "Reading the News with Netscape."

- *Download files from FTP sites*. FTP is another way to get information off of the Internet. You can use Netscape to get files by FTP. You can find a wide variety of free and shareware software on FTP sites that you can download and use. You can also find text files, pictures, and more on FTP sites. This is covered in Part VIII, "FTP, Gopher, and E-mail."

- *Send mail on the Internet*. With this latest release, Netscape now includes a full-featured e-mail program. E-mail with Netscape is also covered in Part VIII. There you will see how to send and read e-mail with Netscape.

- *Shop online*. With Netscape, you can connect to sites that sell their goods and order them online. Or if you aren't in a buying mood, you can just browse and see what is available. You can use the same methods to search for information and get feedback from online databases. Part IX, "What's Hot on the Web," will introduce you to a great shopping site for computer books and many other great sites of all types.

This book is not about the Internet; it is about Netscape. If you need a book about all of the different parts of the Internet and software to use with it, check out the following books from Que:

- *Easy Internet* is a very good book for beginners with the same task style as *Easy World Wide Web with Netscape*. It includes a 3 1/2" disk with software to connect to the Internet. This book is especially good for Windows 3.1 users.

- *Using the Internet with Windows 95* is a good book for casual users with explanations and procedures showing the basic Internet tasks. It includes a 3 1/2" disk with software to connect to the Internet.

- *Special Edition Using the Internet, 2nd Edition*, is a comprehensive book for Windows 3.1 users who want a complete and thorough reference book on all parts of the Internet. It includes a CD-ROM with over 100 programs for connecting to and using the Internet. There is also a new version, Special Edition *Using the Internet with Windows 95*, for Windows 95 users.

You can find these Que books in the computer section at most bookstores or in the books section at your local computer store. If you can't find one there, you can call and order one directly from Que at 1-800-428-5331.

Introduction

Task Sections

The task sections include numbered steps that tell you how to accomplish certain tasks, such as jumping to a page on the Web or viewing a picture. The numbered steps will walk you through a specific example so you can learn the task by actually doing it.

Big Screen

At the beginning of each task is a large screen that shows you how the computer screen will look at some key point in the task. Sometimes, this will show what the screen looks like when you are finished. Other times, it will be an important step along the way.

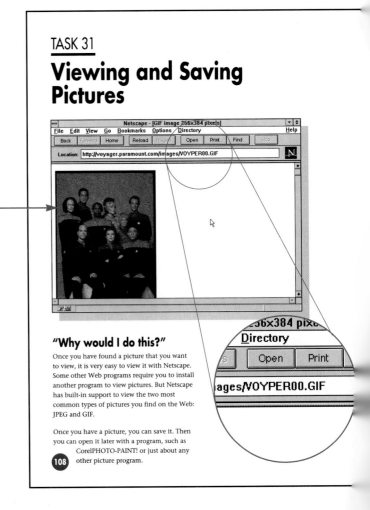

TASK 31

Viewing and Saving Pictures

"Why would I do this?"

Once you have found a picture that you want to view, it is very easy to view it with Netscape. Some other Web programs require you to install another program to view pictures. But Netscape has built-in support to view the two most common types of pictures you find on the Web: JPEG and GIF.

Once you have a picture, you can save it. Then you can open it later with a program, such as CorelPHOTO-PAINT! or just about any other picture program.

108

Step-by-Step Screens

Each task includes a screen shot for each numbered step of a procedure. The screen shot shows how the computer screen looks at each step in the process.

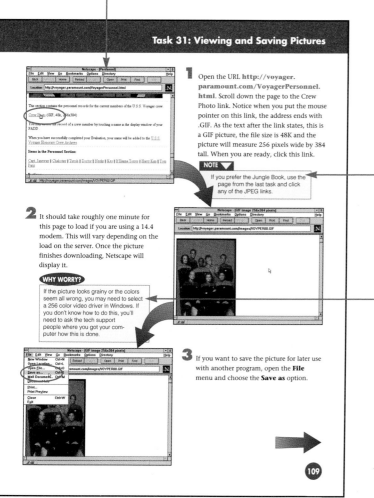

Task 31: Viewing and Saving Pictures

1 Open the URL **http://voyager. paramount.com/VoyagerPersonnel. html**. Scroll down the page to the Crew Photo link. Notice when you put the mouse pointer on this link, the address ends with .GIF. As the text after the link states, this is a GIF picture, the file size is 48K and the picture will measure 256 pixels wide by 384 tall. When you are ready, click this link.

NOTE ▼
If you prefer the Jungle Book, use the page from the last task and click any of the JPEG links.

2 It should take roughly one minute for this page to load if you are using a 14.4 modem. This will vary depending on the load on the server. Once the picture finishes downloading, Netscape will display it.

WHY WORRY?
If the picture looks grainy or the colors seem all wrong, you may need to select a 256 color video driver in Windows. If you don't know how to do this, you'll need to ask the tech support people where you got your computer how this is done.

3 If you want to save the picture for later use with another program, open the **File** menu and choose the **Save as** option.

Notes and Tips

Many tasks include Notes or Tips that tell you a little more about a procedure or alert you to a time-saving shortcut.

Why Worry? Notes

You may find that you performed a task, such as jumping to another page on the Web following the numbered steps, but that the results didn't turn out the way you expected. The Why Worry? notes tell you what common problems you may expect or how to proceed if something didn't work as planned.

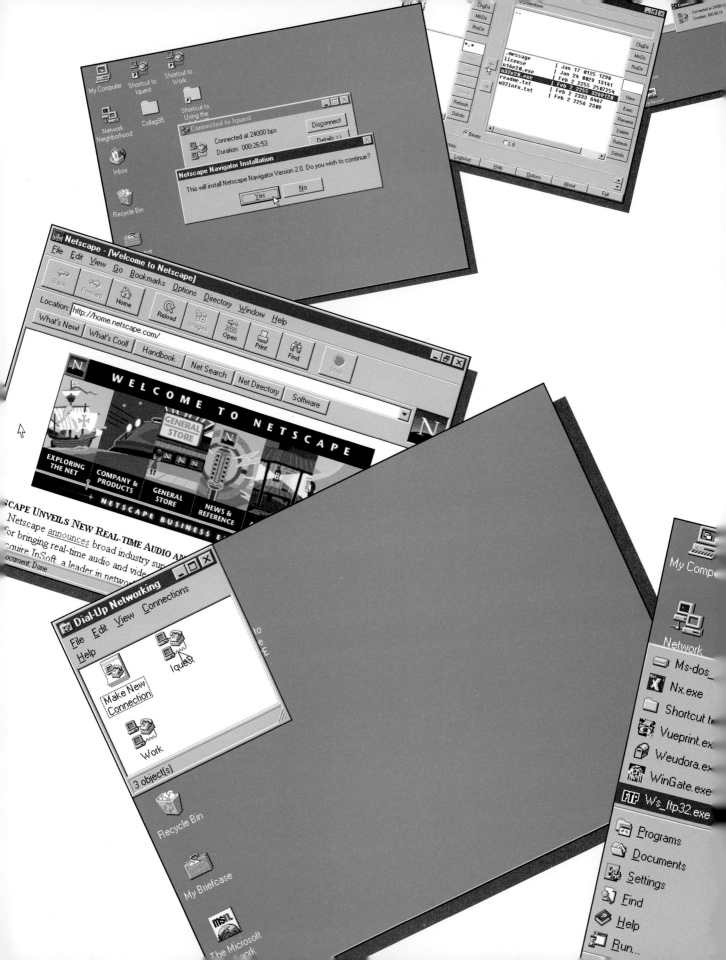

PART I

Getting Up and Running with Netscape

Part I of this book introduces you to Netscape Navigator 2.0 (Netscape for short) and the World Wide Web. This part will show you where to get Netscape, how to install it, and how to get started once you have it installed.

The World Wide Web is part of the Internet. The Internet is a large computer network that connects computers all over the world. By some estimates, as many as 50 million people have access to the Internet. The Internet can be used to send and receive e-mail, read news, send and receive files, and connect to the World Wide Web.

The World Wide Web is a collection of documents from all over the world. These documents can contain more than just text. A document could contain text, pictures, sound, and even movies. This combination of elements is called *multimedia*.

The multimedia elements of the Web are one of the things that have made the Web so popular. But the primary draw of the Web is the way it links the documents together. Imagine that you're reading a book and in the middle of the book, the author mentions another book. So, you hop in your car and drive to the bookstore because this other book sounds interesting. They don't have the book so you call a few other bookstores until you find one that has the book. You get back home, read a few pages in the new book, and this book refers to a favorite movie of yours. Because it's a favorite, you've got it on tape and you pop it in the VCR and watch it for a while.

This is something like what the Internet is usually like. You go one place for text, another for video, and none of them are connected. But the Web draws all of these documents from all over the world together with *hypertext*. When an author creates a document on the Web, the document can contain links to any other Web document. Then, when you click on one of these links, that new document is opened. A single Web page can contain links to pages from all over the world.

So how do you access this world of information? You need a program that is a Web browser and that's where Netscape comes in. Netscape is the most popular Web browser available. We're going to be looking at the version of Netscape that runs in Windows, although many of the tasks in this book will apply to other computers running Netscape too.

But, before you can get Netscape and run it, the following requirements for your computer must be met:

- First, you need to have **Windows 3.1** or Windows 95 running on your computer. For Windows 3.1, your computer needs at least 4 Mb RAM and at least 5 Mb of free space on the hard drive. (You'll be much better off if you have more RAM and more free hard drive space.) For Windows 95, you will need at least 8MB RAM and 10MB of free hard drive space.

- A 9600 bps or faster **modem** (a 14,400 bps modem is recommended and a 28,800 bps modem is best).

- Next, you need to have a **connection to the Internet** through a modem or a network at your office. (If you are lucky enough to have a connection through a network, you don't need a modem.)

The kind of connection you will need to connect to the Internet uses a small but important piece of software called a **Winsock** (short for Windows Sockets). This software creates the connection to the Internet that allows Windows-based Internet applications like Netscape to work.

Windows 95 users are in the best shape when it comes to setting up their Winsock. Windows 95 has a built in Winsock that is very easy to configure and use. If you need help with some of the technical parts of this process, consult your Internet service provider or a book like *Using the Internet with Windows 95* or *Special Edition Using the Internet with Windows 95*.

Windows 3.1 users should not despair, though. There are many software packages available at your local computer store or electronics superstore that will provide everything you need to connect to the Internet. You may want to ask your Internet service provider which one they recommend. If you don't already have a provider in mind, most of these sofware packages come with everything you need to connect to one of several major providers and many offer special discounted rates.

Another way is to find a book that includes software for connecting to the Internet. The advantage of this is that you get the software you need and a book that shows you how to use it. All of the books listed in the intro-duction of this book include software to connect to the Internet. Read the descriptions there or take a look at them at your local bookstore to determine which one best matches your needs.

Once you have your software to connect to the Internet, you're ready to explore the Web with Netscape.

Opening Your Internet Connection

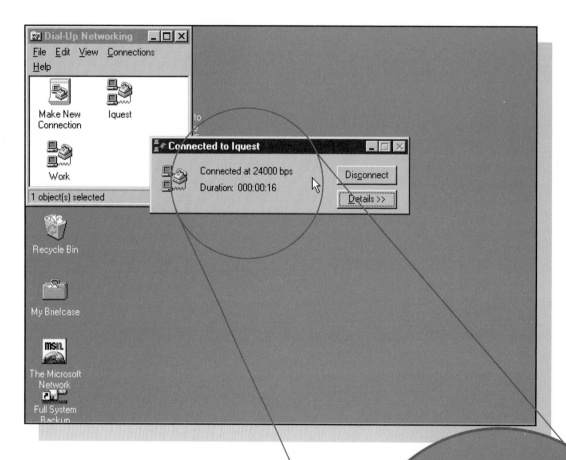

"Why would I do this?"

Before you can cruise the Web, you've got to be connected to the Internet. To do this in Windows 3.1 or 95, you start a program called a Winsock. (In Windows 95, this is part of Dial-Up Networking.) Regardless of which one you use, it will dial your modem and log you in with your service provider.

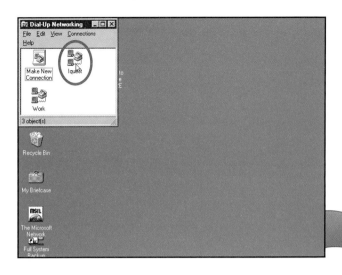

1 Start Windows and open the Dial-Up Networking folder. Then double-click the shortcut for your service provider.

WHY WORRY?

The steps and screens here show Windows 95. If you are using Windows 3.1, follow your software's procedure to connect to the Internet.

2 Enter your User Name, password, and any other needed information, then click connect.

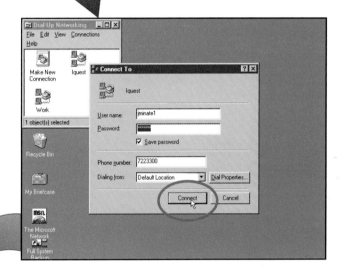

3 After the Winsock dials in, you should see a message that tells you that the login was successful and that you are connected to the Internet. This message will be different depending on your software or service provider.

WHY WORRY?

If you don't get connected, don't worry; just try again.

TASK 2

Getting a Copy of Netscape by FTP

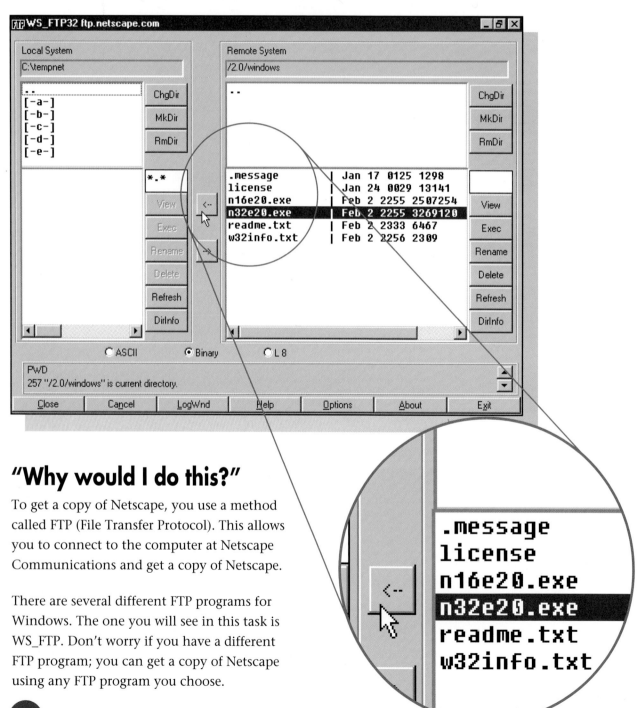

"Why would I do this?"

To get a copy of Netscape, you use a method called FTP (File Transfer Protocol). This allows you to connect to the computer at Netscape Communications and get a copy of Netscape.

There are several different FTP programs for Windows. The one you will see in this task is WS_FTP. Don't worry if you have a different FTP program; you can get a copy of Netscape using any FTP program you choose.

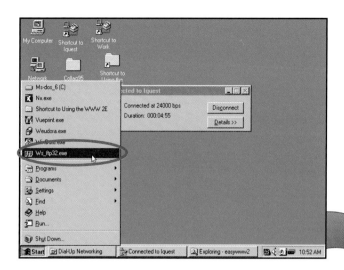

1 With your Winsock and Internet connection running (you started this in Task 1), start your FTP program.

NOTE ▼

Windows 95 users can use the built in FTP command in Windows 95 if you don't have a graphical FTP program.

2 In ws_ FTP, click **New** to create a new entry for Netscape.

NOTE ▼

By creating a new profile and saving it, you can easily connect to Netscape Communications again at a later time. This is useful if you want to see if there is a new version of the program or if anything happens to your copy and you need to get the program again.

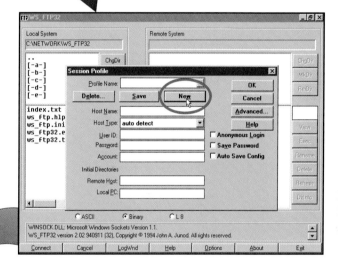

3 In the Profile Name box, type **Netscape**. In the Host Name box type **ftp.netscape.com**. Click the **Anonymous Login** box. Click **Save** to save this entry.

4 Click **OK** to start a connection to Netscape Communications. This may take anywhere from a few seconds to a minute. You should see messages that you are connecting and logging in.

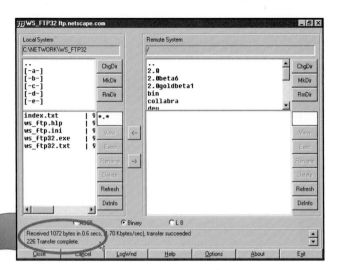

WHY WORRY?

If you get an error message and don't connect, you probably didn't do anything wrong. The Netscape Communications site is probably too busy. Click Connect, be sure the information is entered correctly, and click OK to try again. Keep trying until you get connected.

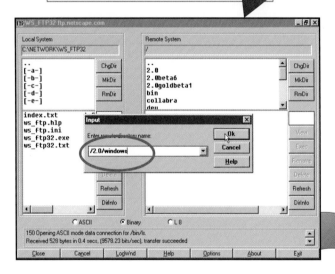

5 Click the **ChgDir** button on the right side of the screen to change directories at the Netscape site. Type **/2.0/windows** as the directory to change to and click **OK**. Click the other **ChgDir** button to change directories on your hard drive. Type the name of an empty temporary directory and click **OK**.

WHY WORRY?

If you don't have an empty temporary directory, it is easy to create one. Click the MkDir button and enter a directory name like \nettemp.

6 Highlight the n32e20.exe and click the left arrow to transfer the Netscape file from Netscape to your computer. (Windows 3.1 users should hightlight n16e20.exe.)

NOTE ▼

If you don't see this exact file name in this directory, there may be a newer version or it may be in a different directory. The file name should be similar but with different last numbers.

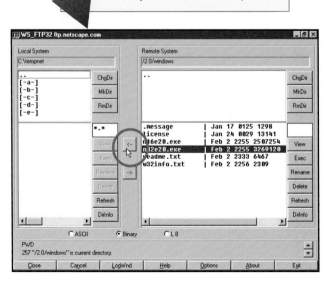

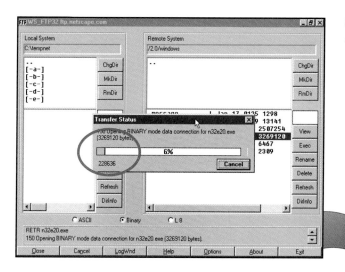

7 A dialog box will open showing you the progress of the file transfer. Depending on the speed of your connection, this can take anywhere from a few seconds (if you are connected through a LAN with a high speed connection) to a little over an hour if you have a 14.4 modem.

8 When the transfer is complete, you will see a message that the file transfer was successful. The file name n32e20.exe will now appear in your local directory, too. Close your connection to Netscape by clicking the **Close** button.

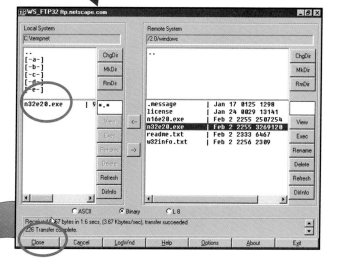

> **NOTE** ▼
>
> Don't leave the connection open for no reason; this keeps other people from being able to connect.

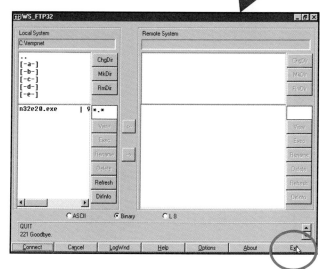

9 After the connection is closed, click **Exit** to exit the FTP program.

TASK 3
Installing Netscape

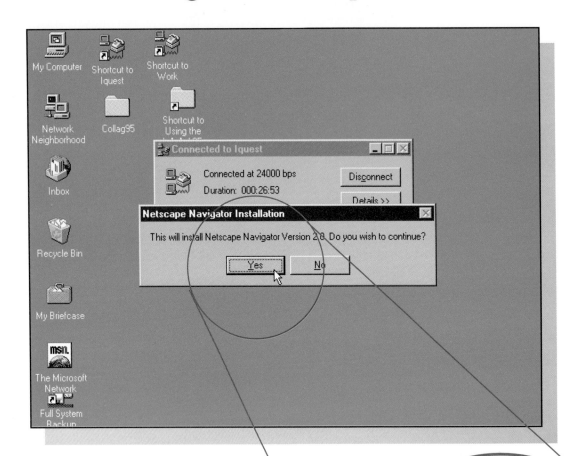

"Why would I do this?"

Once you have a copy of the Netscape program, you still have to install it before it is ready to run. The file that you transferred with FTP is compressed to save time transferring it. Part of the installation process will expand this compressed file. The other part will create a program group and icon for Netscape.

Before beginning, be sure you have at least 5Mb of free disk space on the drive you are going to install Netscape on. You'll get some of this space back after the installation is complete, but you'll need it all while installing.

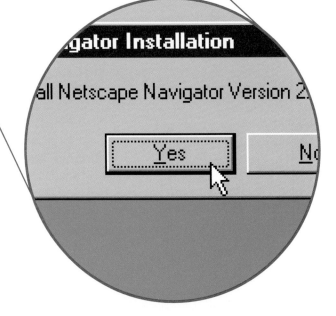

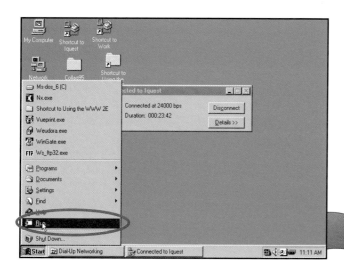

1 In Windows, open the **Start** menu and choose **Run**.

2 In the Run dialog box, type **c:\tempnet\n32e20.exe**. If you transferred the file to a different drive or directory, use that drive letter or directory instead. If the file name you transferred is different, substitute that name here. After typing this, press **Enter** or click **OK**. This will begin decompressing the file you downloaded.

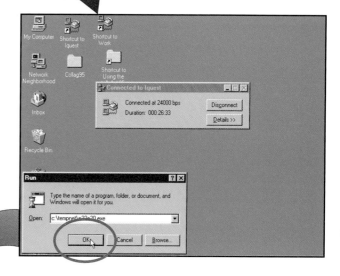

3 After a few message dialogs flash by, a dialog box will prompt you to continue. Click Yes.

4 After that, you will see the Welcome dialog box. To continue the installation, click **Next**.

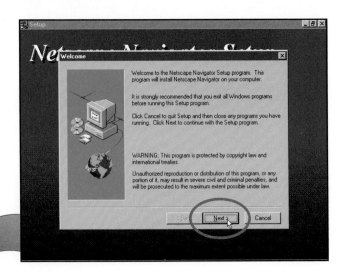

5 The next dialog box, Netscape Setup: Installation Location, prompts you for a location where you want to install Netscape. If you don't want to install this in the default directory, enter a new directory name. When you have chosen a directory, click **Next**.

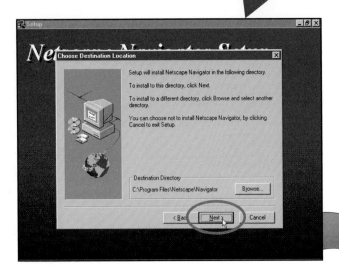

6 As this installation progresses, you will see a dialog box showing the percentage of the files that have been installed.

WHY WORRY?

Some users have reported problems installing Netscape when they were running programs such as Norton Desktop for Windows or PC Tools for Windows that run over Windows. If you use one of these, be sure to run the installation from Program Manager.

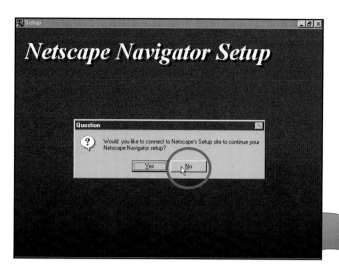

7 The next message you will see asks you if you want to connect to Netscape's setup site. You can click No here.

8 When you see the message that setup is complete, click OK.

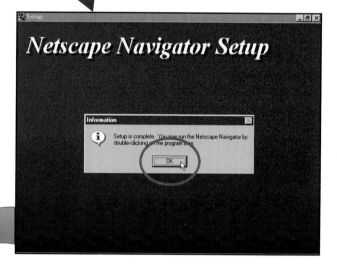

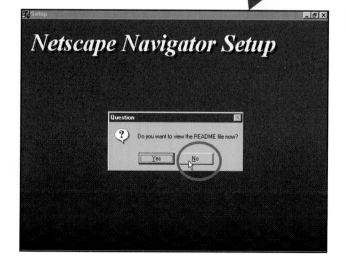

9 The last message you will see asks you if you want to see a README file. You can skip this by clicking No.

Starting and Exiting Netscape

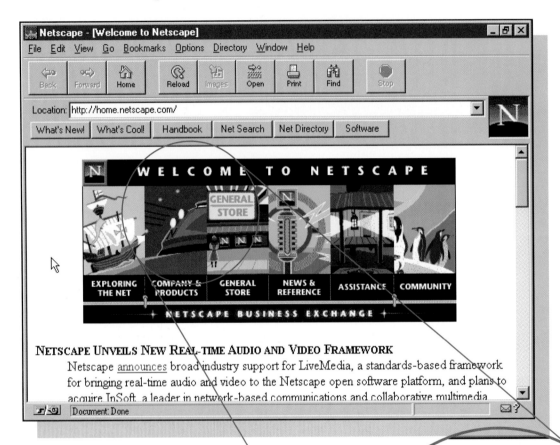

"Why would I do this?"

Once Netscape has been installed, you are ready
to start the program. You will see a few extra
dialog boxes that state the Netscape license
policy. After you read these once and agree, you
won't see them again when you start Netscape.
Although you can download and try Netscape
for free, it is not free for continued use for all
users. Be sure to read the agreement to see if
you are required to pay to use it. Once you
know how to start the program, you'll also want
to exit it when you are done.

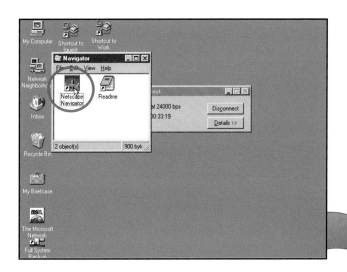

1 With your Winsock program running and your connection to the Internet open, double-click the Netscape icon in Windows.

NOTE ▼

Netscape Communications has used several different program icons for Netscape since they introduced Netscape. Don't be surprised if your icon looks a little different than the one here.

2 Read the license agreement and click **Accept** if you agree to the terms.

NOTE ▼

If you're anxious to get started cruising the Web, you don't have to exit now. Just skip step 3 and move on to Part II of the book.

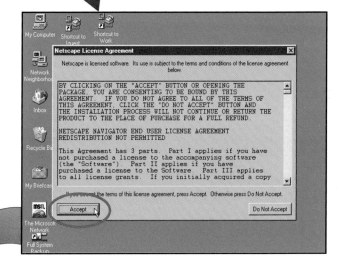

3 After accepting the program license agreement, Netscape will start. When the Welcome page loads, you have successfully started.

To exit Netscape, open the **File** menu and choose **Exit**. If you are done with your Internet connection, you should also close your Winsock program.

Navigating the Web with Netscape

WORLD WIDE WEB

In Part I, you connected to the Internet and got a copy of Netscape. You installed it, started it, and entered some information about yourself. With that out of the way, you're ready to begin your exploration of the Web.

When you first start Netscape, you'll be connected to the *home page* at Netscape Communications. Home page is used to describe two similar things. First, the document that Netscape connects to when you start it is called your home page.

Second, when you connect to a *Web site*, the main page there is often called the home page. This can be a little confusing, but most of the time you'll know which of these meanings we're referring to. A Web site is a computer on the Internet that a company, university, government office, individual, or any other organization has put all of their Web pages on. With Netscape, you connect to Web sites and view their pages.

When you have a page open in Netscape, there will be *hyperlinks* you use to open other pages. These hyperlinks can be highlighted text or even graphics. You can move to other pages by clicking on one of these links. You can also move to other documents by going back to a page you've already had open.

Every page on the Web has a unique address. These addresses are called *Uniform Resource Locators*, or URLs. (URL is pronounced like Earl.) If you know a page's URL, you can open it without having to go through other pages to get there. An URL looks like the following:

http://www.mcp.com/que/que.html

Here's how you interpret an URL. The first part, **http://** in this case, tells what kind of a server the URL will open. **http://** is the beginning for Web servers, which hold most of the documents you will load in Netscape.

The next part, **www.mcp.com**, is the Internet address for the Web site where the document is located.

After that, the **/que** tells you that the document is in the **/que** directory on the server. Notice that the slash here is a forward slash / instead of the backslash \ used by DOS and Windows.

The final part of the address tells the filename of the exact document the URL will open. Keep in mind that these filenames can be longer than filenames in Windows and DOS. Filenames may also have characters that aren't allowed in DOS.

The extension in this case, **.html**, tells you what type of file it is. Web documents are written in a format called HTML. This format includes the text of the Web document and special codes that tell Netscape how to format the document, where any graphic images go, and so forth.

Remember to always enter an URL exactly as it's given, including upper- and lowercase letters. If you don't enter the URL exactly, it won't load.

In this part we'll show you how you can change the home page that Netscape loads for you. We'll also show you how you can open more than one window at a time so that you can have more than one page open at once.

One of the big uses for the Web that many businesses and consumers are discovering is how to buy and sell goods and services on the Web. In the past, many people have been afraid to give out their credit card numbers to companies on the Web. After all, the Web is part of the Internet and many stories have been written about how many hackers and data thieves make their home on the Net. But thanks to Netscape, you can safely give out credit card information, or anything else private, on the Web. Netscape has built-in security and if you connect to a site that is secure, you can safely give them any information. We'll show you how to know if the site you are connected to is secure.

Jumping to a Link

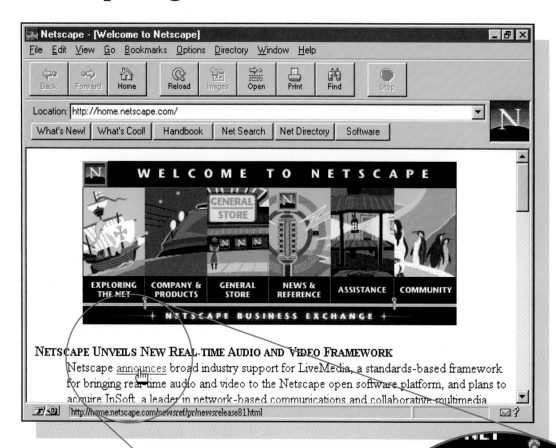

"Why would I do this?"

The whole point of the Web centers around
the links from one document to another. In
Netscape, these links show up as blue text by
default. Links can also be graphics. A graphic
that is a link has a blue border around it.

When you click on one of the links, Netscape
loads the document that is connected to that
link. That document can be another Web
page or a file of any type. In this part, we'll
concentrate on the first type of link—a link
to another Web page.

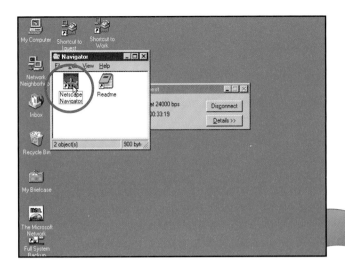

1 If Netscape isn't already running, double-click the Netscape icon to start it.

NOTE ▼

If you want to change the page that Netscape loads when it starts, see Task 10, "Changing Your Home Page."

2 As Netscape starts, it begins by loading the home page. As the page loads, the status bar at the bottom of the screen will tell you what Netscape is doing. Netscape will look for the host, connect to it, wait for a reply, then load the document. As the document loads, watch the red bar at the right end of the status bar. This bar gives a visual indication of how much of the document has loaded.

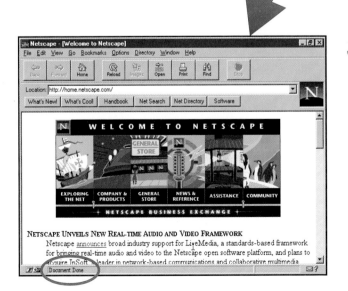

3 After the text of the page loads, you can scroll through the page while the graphics load. There will be empty spaces where the graphic will be when they load. Netscape will load quick, blurry versions at first, then the details will be filled in and the images will be clearer. When the graphics and text finish loading, the status bar message will be "Document: Done." The title bar will contain the name of the page and the location bar will contain the page's address.

4 Scroll down through the document and look for a link that seems interesting. When you put the mouse pointer over a link, the pointer changes to a hand. While the pointer is over the link, the URL address for the link is shown in the status bar. Click the mouse button on the link and that page will load.

NOTE ▼

Watch the Netscape icon;comets fly by as the page loads.

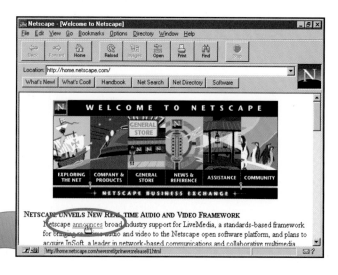

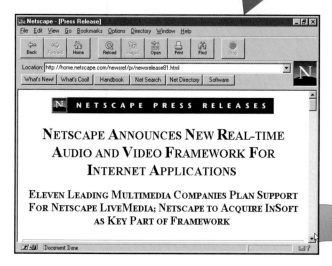

5 After a few seconds (or minutes, depending on the size of the page and the speed of your Internet connection) the new page will load. You can now scroll through this page and look for another link to jump to.

WHY WORRY?

If the status indicators stop, or you see a message like "Connecting To Host" for several minutes and nothing else happens, the site with the page you are loading may be too busy or not working. If this happens and you get tired of waiting, click the Stop button.

6 Scroll through this page and click on any other link you want. (The circled link here will take you back to the page we just came from.)

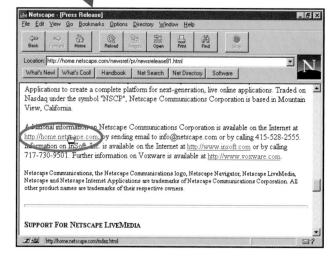

Going to a Page by Entering the Address or by Clicking an Image

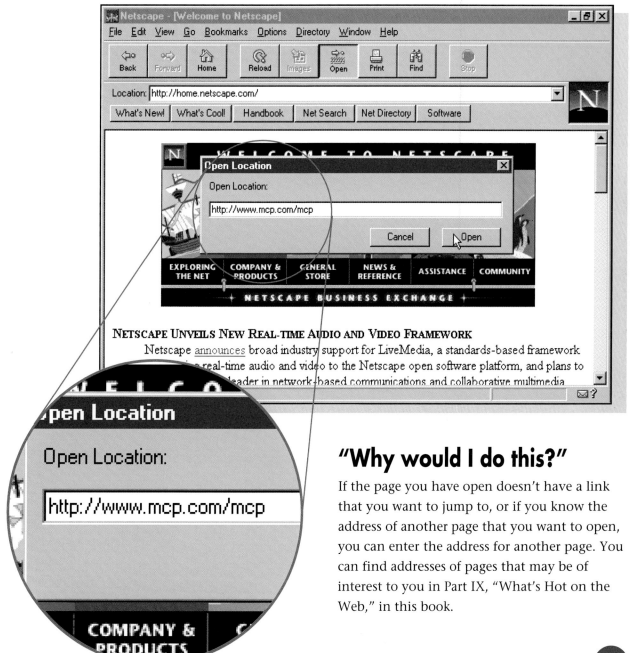

"Why would I do this?"

If the page you have open doesn't have a link that you want to jump to, or if you know the address of another page that you want to open, you can enter the address for another page. You can find addresses of pages that may be of interest to you in Part IX, "What's Hot on the Web," in this book.

1 With any Web page loaded in Netscape, click the **Open** button.

2 In the Open Location dialog box, type the complete address for the page you want to open such as **http://www.mcp.com /mcp**, the home page for Macmillan Computer Publishing. (Be sure to use the forward slash mark /.) After typing in the address, press **Enter** or click **Open**.

TIP ▼

You can also enter the address directly in the Location bar.

3 If you typed in the address correctly, the new page will open. Scroll down until you see the QUE logo. This is part of an *imagemap*. By clicking on the various parts of the imagemap, in this case the various logos, you will direct Netscape to load different pages. To follow along, click the QUE logo.

WHY WORRY?

If the page doesn't load, check the address to be sure it is correct.

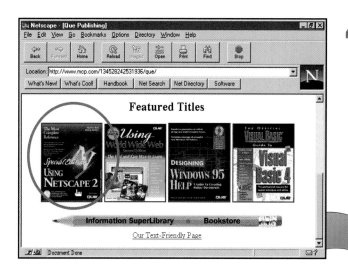

4 When the QUE page loads, scroll to the bottom and look at the pictures there. Each picture is surrounded by a blue box. That box indicates that each picture is a link to another page. Anywhere you click in one of those pictures, takes you to the page the picture is linked to . Click any one of these.

5 The page that's loaded here is the one linked to the book cover you click on, in this case *Special Edition Using Netscape 2.*

> **NOTE** ▼
>
> When you move your mouse pointer over different parts of an image map, watch the Netscape status bar. You will see the message there change as you pass over different parts of the image.

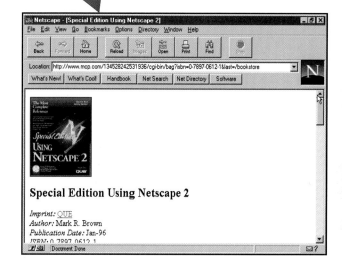

Moving Forward and Backward

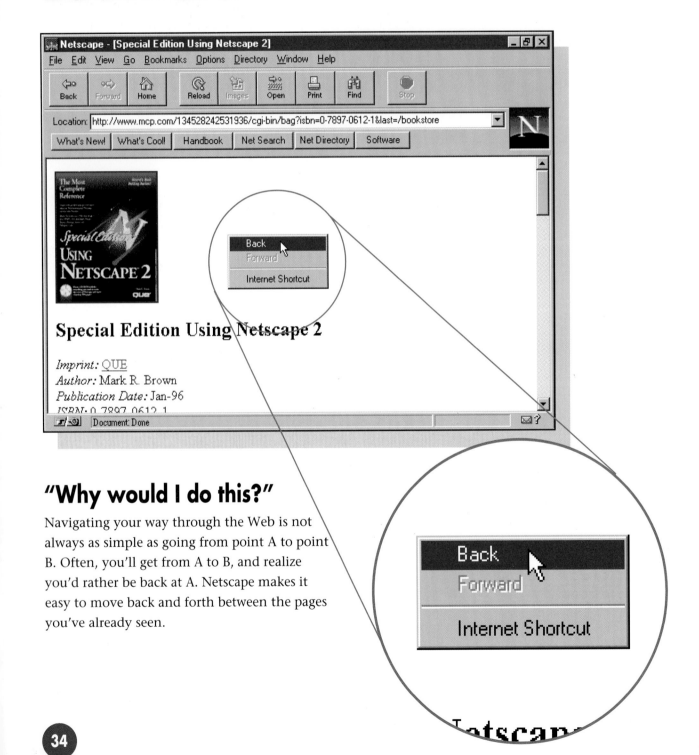

"Why would I do this?"

Navigating your way through the Web is not always as simple as going from point A to point B. Often, you'll get from A to B, and realize you'd rather be back at A. Netscape makes it easy to move back and forth between the pages you've already seen.

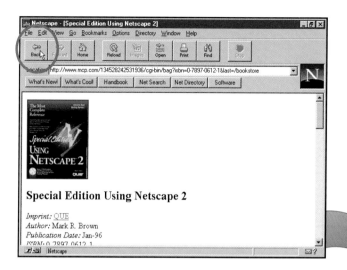

1 If you have clicked on several links and want to get back to one of the earlier ones, click the **Back** button. This will take you to the last page you had open. You can click this repeatedly and go back through all of the pages you have had open.

> **NOTE** ▼
>
> When you get to the first document you had open when you started Netscape, the Back button will be dimmed and you can't go back any further.

2 If, after moving back, you want to go forward again to one of the pages you have already seen, you don't have to click back through the links to get to it. You can click the **Forward** button to move forward through the links you have already seen.

> **NOTE** ▼
>
> The Forward button is only available after you have moved back first. Once you move all the way forward through the links you have seen, you can't move forward anymore.

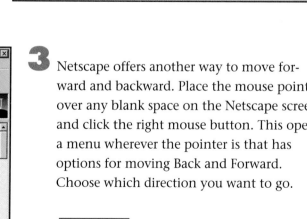

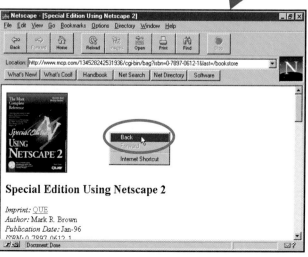

3 Netscape offers another way to move forward and backward. Place the mouse pointer over any blank space on the Netscape screen and click the right mouse button. This opens a menu wherever the pointer is that has options for moving Back and Forward. Choose which direction you want to go.

> **NOTE** ▼
>
> Later you'll see how to remove the toolbar buttons from the screen and this popup menu will come in handy.

Returning to a Recently Used Page

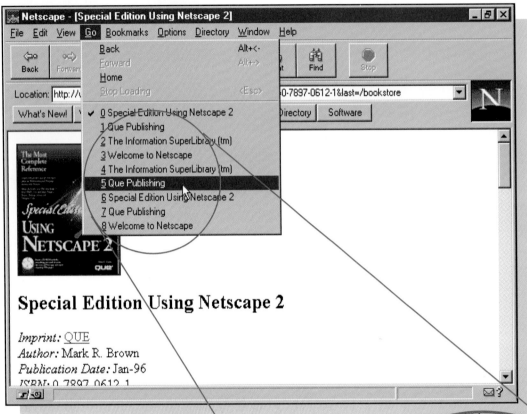

"Why would I do this?"

In addition to being able to move backward and forward through the pages you have seen before, Netscape adds the pages you have seen most recently to the bottom of the Go menu. You can open this menu and choose one of these pages to open it directly, without having to move forward and backward through the pages you have already seen.

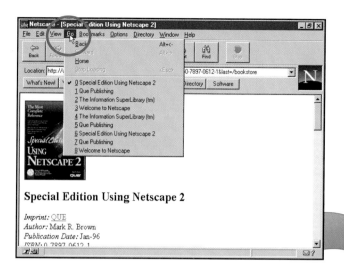

1 Open the **Go** menu. At the bottom of the menu, there should be a list of all the pages you have opened. The page you are at now will be at the top of the list with a checkmark and the number 0 by it. The rest of the pages you have open will be below it in reverse order (the first document you loaded will be at the bottom).

2 To open one of the pages on this list, click on it in the list. If it is one of the numbered pages, you can press Alt and the number to open it (just like you use Alt with the other underlined keys on menus in Windows).

> **NOTE** ▼
>
> Up to 10 of the most recent documents will be numbered, starting with 0 numbered up to 9. The rest of the documents won't have numbers.

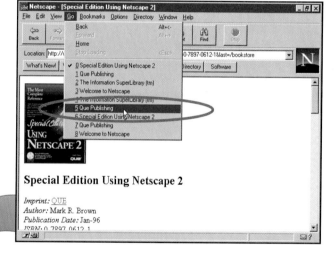

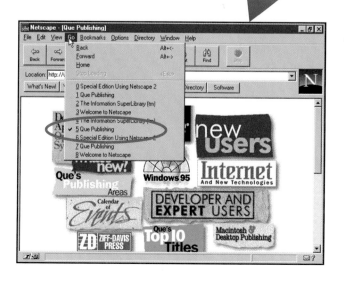

3 After opening the pages, open the **Go** menu again. The checkmark is now by the page you picked from the list but the list hasn't been reordered. Netscape keeps this list in the order you first visited the pages in this session.

> **WHY WORRY?**
>
> If you have opened several pages, then use this list to jump back to a page near the beginning of the list, some of the more recent links will disappear.

Moving to Your Home Page

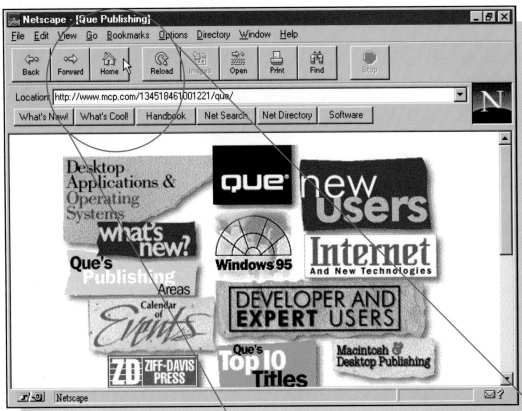

"Why would I do this?"

It's easy to get lost on the Web. Your travels can take you to pages all over the world and far from where you started. It's times like this that it's nice to be able to get back to some page that you are familiar with to help you find your bearings. For most people, this is their home page. Once you are at your home page, you are back where you started and should be able to find your way again.

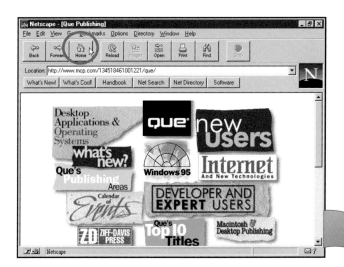

1 To move to your home page from any other page, click the **Home** button.

2 You will now be at your home page. By default, this is Netscape's Welcome to Netscape page.

> **TIP** ▼
>
> The next task will show you how to change which page Netscape uses as your home page.

TASK 10

Changing Your Home Page

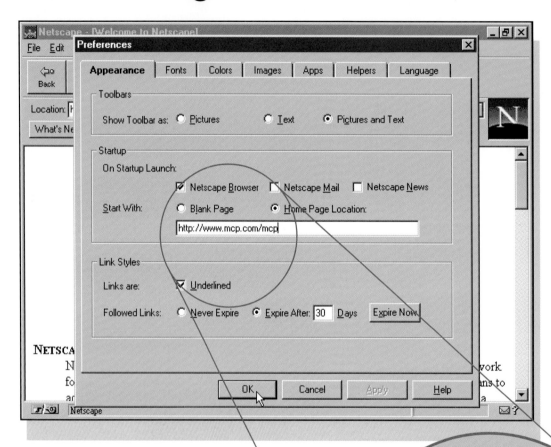

"Why would I do this?"

By default, the home for Netscape is set to be the Welcome to Netscape page on the Netscape Communications site. Each time you start Netscape or click the home button, this is the page that will open.

But what if you have another page that you use more often? Maybe your company has a Web site and you want to always start your Web sessions from there. If that's the case, you'll want to change your home page.

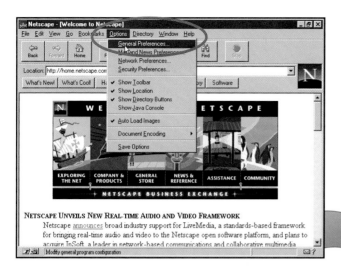

1 Open the **Options** menu and choose General **Preferences**.

2 Click the Appearances tab at the top left of the dialog box. In the Startup part of the box, enter the URL address of the page you want to make your home page. Be sure the **Home Page Location** option is selected. When you have entered the address, click **OK**.

NOTE ▼

If you don't want any page to open when you start Netscape, select the Blank Page option instead of Home Page Location. No page will open when you start but your home page will still load when you click Home.

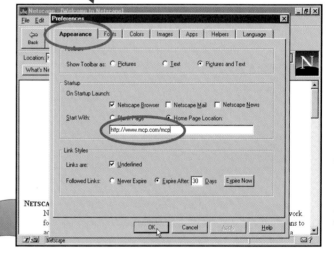

3 Open the **Options** menu and choose **Save Options**. This will save your home page choice. The next time you start Netscape or click Home, this new page will open.

Opening Another Window

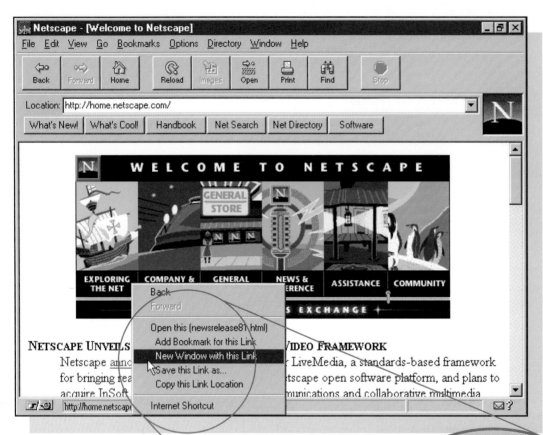

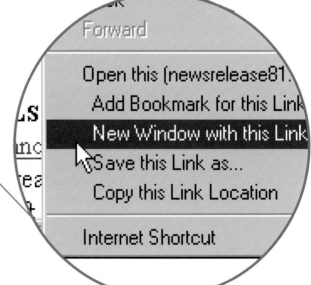

"Why would I do this?"

If you want to follow two different links from the same page, you can open a second window in Netscape. With two windows open, you can follow a different path on the Web in each one.

Once you have two windows open, you can move and resize them to see what you want on-screen.

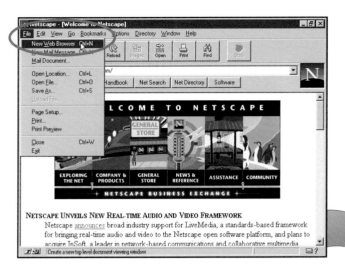

1 Open the **File** menu and choose the **New Web Browser** option.

2 The page that opens in the new window will be the last page that you opened in Netscape. You can then resize and arrange the windows so you can see both of them on-screen. You can now open different links in the two different windows so, in effect, you can go in two directions at once.

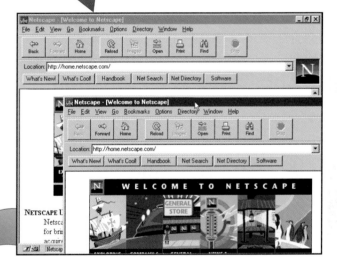

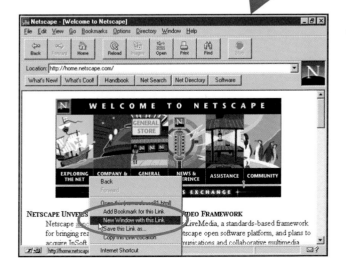

3 If you want to jump to a new page from a link and open it into a new window in one step, place the mouse pointer over the link and click the right button to open the shortcut menu. Choose the **New Window with this Link** option. A new window will open from this link.

Connecting to Secure Sites

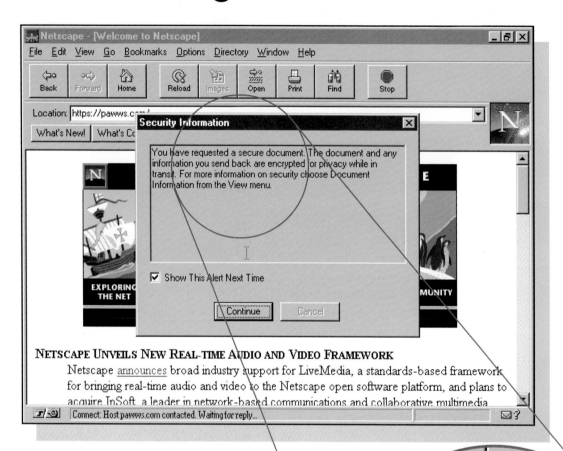

"Why would I do this?"

One of the explosive and exciting new uses of the Web is online business. There are Web pages where you can order goods and services from all over the world online, but ordering from many of these sites requires sending the business your credit card and other personal information over the Web. Or maybe you want to fill out an online survey form, but you don't want others to read your responses. This information could be intercepted and read by others if the site isn't secure. This section will show you how to determine if the site you are sending the information to is secure.

1 Look at the bottom of the page you have open. At the far left side of the status bar, there is a key icon. If this key is broken, the site isn't secure.

To see what a secure site looks like, click the **Open** button.

2 Enter the URL address **https://powws.com** in the Open Location dialog box and then press **Enter** or click **Open**. This is the address for a secure, online financial network.

> **TIP** ▼
>
> If you don't want to see this dialog box each time you connect to a secure site, click the Show This Alert Next Time option to remove the X.

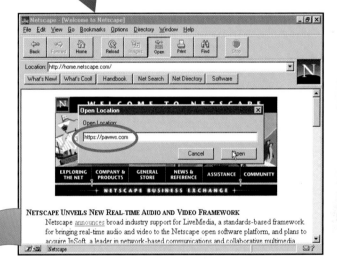

3 If you see a message like the one shown here, it means that the site you are connecting to probably has not configured their name correctly in their security software. Most likely, there is nothing amiss but there is a slim chance that someone is trying to intercept information you send to this site. Here, you have the option of canceling or continuing.

4 The next screen you see will be the Security Information dialog box. read this dialog box and then click **Continue**.

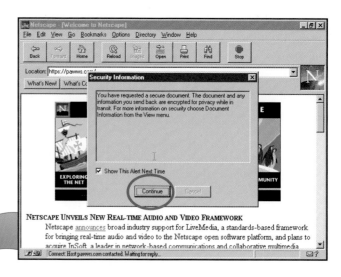

5 When the page at the secure site opens, notice that the key icon isn't broken. You should also see a blue bar at the top of the document area. These bars are gray for unsecure documents.

6 When you are ready to leave this secure site, you can enter the address for any other site in the Location bar using the Open Location command. If the site you connect to next does not use security (and most don't) you'll see a message letting you know that you are leaving a secure area.

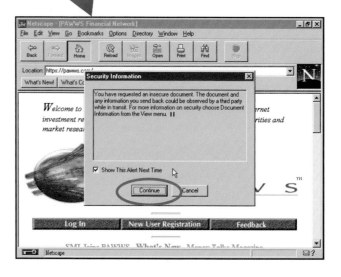

Customizing What You See On-screen

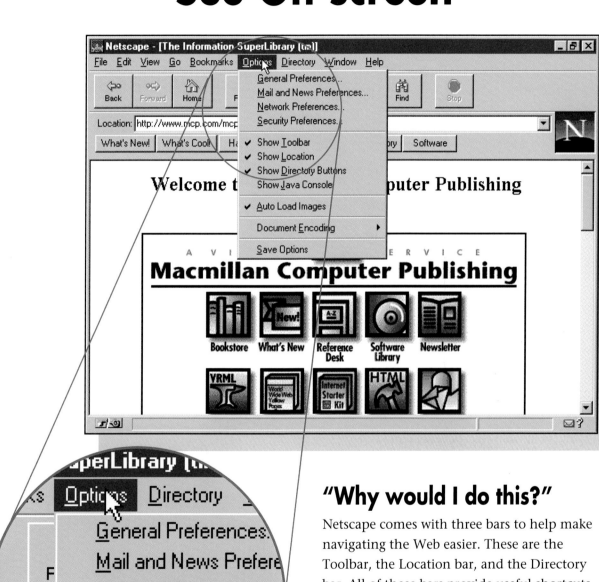

"Why would I do this?"

Netscape comes with three bars to help make navigating the Web easier. These are the Toolbar, the Location bar, and the Directory bar. All of these bars provide useful shortcuts for common tasks or information about where you are on the Web.

But, they also take up space on the screen and limit the amount of a page you can see. If you don't use some of these bars often and would rather be able to see more of the Web pages on-screen at once, you can customize which bars you see.

47

1 Open the **Options** menu. The three bars are controlled by options on this menu. These are the Show Toolbar, Show Location, and Show Directory Buttons options. By default, these are all checked. To change the display so that any of these isn't shown, select the option from the menu. This will remove the checkmark and remove the bar from your screen.

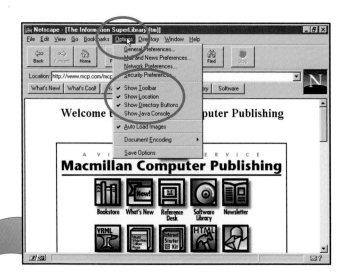

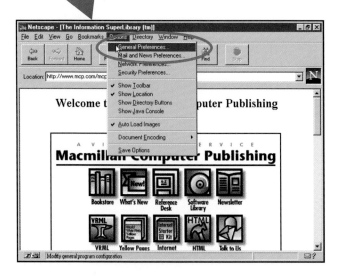

2 After turning off all of these bars, you will have much more room on-screen to see Web pages. When you have decided which bars you use often, turn them back on.

NOTE ▼

Another way to make more room on-screen is to change your Windows display. Many Netscape users prefer to use 800x600 screen resolution. If you know how to change resolutions in Windows, you may want to try this or another higher resolution.

3 You also have more precise control over the Toolbar and what is shown on it. Open the **Options** menu and choose **General Preferences**.

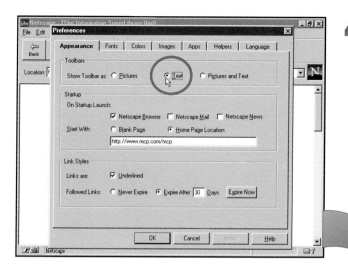

4 To make the buttons on the Toolbar smaller, you can select either the **Pictures** or **Text** options. This will make the buttons display either the Pictures or Text instead of both, which is the default.

WHY WORRY?

If the dialog box doesn't look like this one, click the Appearance tab at the upper left of the dialog box.

5 Another option you may want to customize is the background color. Some people find the gray background a little difficult to look at. If you have another color you prefer, you can change it.

At the top of the dialog box, click the Color tab.

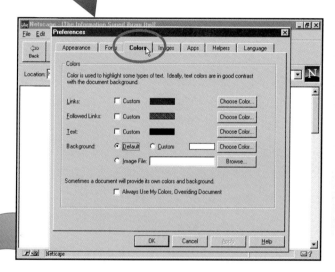

6 Near the bottom of the dialog box, click the **Choose Color** button that is aligned with Background, Default, and Custom.

NOTE ▼

You can use this same general process to change the color of the links or text on-screen by clicking one of the other Choose Color buttons.

7 Click on the color you want to use for a background. The color you click will have a little border around it. After you choose the color, click **OK** in the Color dialog box.

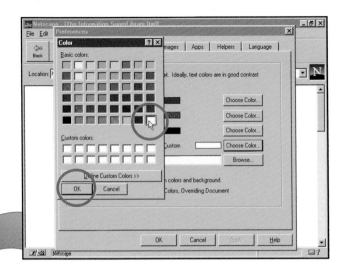

8 Click **OK** in the Preferences dialog box.

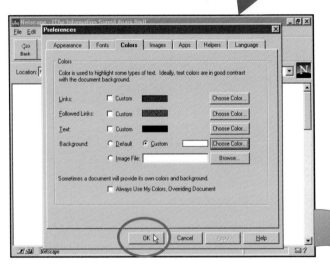

> **TIP**
>
> Some web pages come with their own background colors, images as backgrounds, and different colors as text and links. If you want to be able to see these when they are part of a page, do not select the Always Use My Colors, Overriding Document option. If you want to use your selections regardless of the document, select it.

9 When you are done making your changes, open the **Options** menu and choose **Save Options**. This will save all of your changes. In this screen, you can see that the Toolbar has the Text option selected and the background is white.

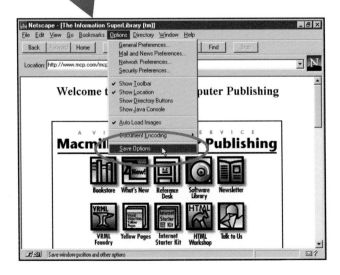

Speeding Netscape by Disabling Images

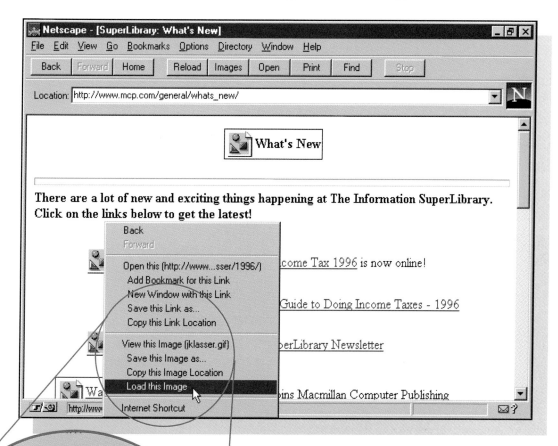

"Why would I do this?"

After you have cruised the Web for a while, you will notice that things aren't always as fast as you want. Netscape has been designed for speed but there are a few things that you can do to make it even faster.

One of the parts of the Web that will really slow you down is the images that are in Web pages. These images can take a long time to download. So, if you don't need to see these pictures for every page, you can save a lot of time.

1 Open the **Options** menu and choose the **Auto Load Images**. By default, there is a checkmark next to this, which means that all of the images in pages will be loaded when you load a page. By choosing this, you will remove the checkmark.

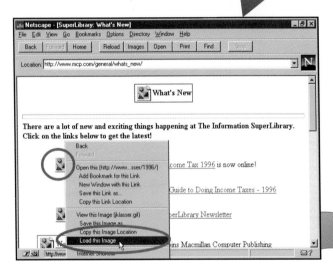

2 Now load another page. When it loads, instead of images, you will just see small icons where the pictures would be. If you want to see any one of the graphics on the page, click on it with the right mouse button and choose the **Load this Image** option from the menu. The image will load.

3 If any of the unloaded images has a thin line around it with text inside the box, you can load it by clicking on it once with the left mouse button. Click it to load the image.

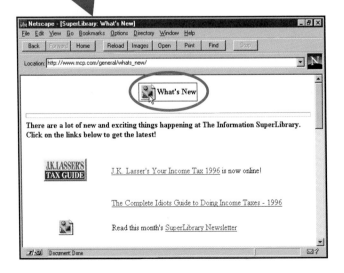

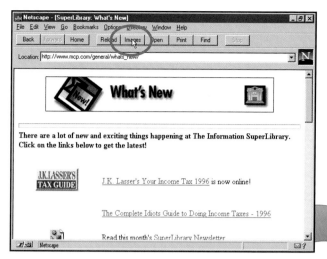

4 Now the image has been loaded.

If you see that there are several images on a page and you want to see them all, you can load all of the images at once. To load all of the images on a page, click the **Images** button.

5 Now all of the images on this page will be loaded.

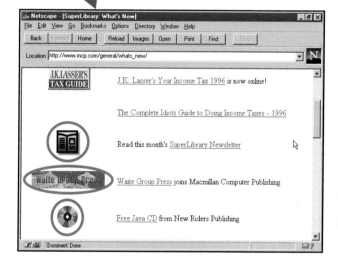

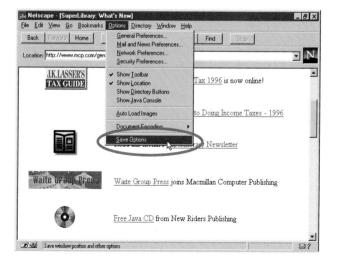

6 Open the Options menu and choose Save Options.

PART III

Finding Your Way on the Web

Now that you know the basics of getting around the Web with Netscape, you're probably anxious to find something of interest. You've read about all of the great resources on the Web, but you don't know where to look. In this part, you'll learn how to find anything you want on the Web.

The Web is huge. There are over twenty million Web pages with information on every imaginable subject. You can find pages with literally everything you want. From A to Z, arts to zoology, it's all out there.

But how can you find it? Many experienced Web users have compared the Web to a library. But this isn't a library like you're familiar with. This library has no card catalog, no librarians, and all of the books are just thrown in the library in random piles. Anyone can bring in a book and throw it on one of the piles.

If you went into a library like this, how would you find anything? You wouldn't. You'd randomly pick up a few books and look through them until you found something interesting. This might be fine if you were just casually browsing, but what if you were looking for something in particular? It could take a long time to find it with no guide to where it is. And at the rate the Web is growing, there's more new information added every day, which makes it even more difficult to find your way around.

Luckily, several individuals and organizations have started to build card catalogs for the Web. None of these are comprehensive; they don't contain listings for every page on the Web.

Some of these lists are like big indexes that you can read through for what you need. They're broken down by categories like arts, entertainment, computers, sports, and more. You look through the index for the category you want, then select the heading. If you select the sports heading for instance, you may see subheadings for various sports such as basketball, baseball, football, and more. Choosing one of these may bring up more subcategories or it may bring up links to individual pages.

The other type of navigational aid to help you find your way on the Web is a search form. These have unusual names like spider, worm, or crawler. (Their creators try to be original.) These go out on the Web and search for Web pages, collect information about them like their titles, subjects, and keywords. The spider (or worm or crawler) reports all of this information back to a database where it is all stored.

All of this stored information is great but you still need a way to search the database. So each of these creatures has a Web page you can interact with. You load the Web page, just like any other page and fill in a form telling it what you're looking for. Maybe you want to find all of the Web pages that have to do with Macmillan Computer Publishing. You might start this search by looking for "Macmillan."

In this part, we'll look at a few of the more well-known search pages and indexes. This should give you a good feel for how they work, how to use them, and what kind of information each one reports back. Some of the searches are more up to date than others, others excel in narrowing down the results to the most likely matches.

In the process, you'll also learn how to use forms on the Web. Forms on the Web are like forms on paper. With a paper form, you fill in the blanks, maybe check a couple of boxes, and then submit the form. It works the same way on the Web except you use Netscape to fill in the form instead of your number 2 pencil. Once your form is filled in and submitted, you should get almost immediate feedback.

WORLD WIDE WEB

TASK 15
The Yahoo Directory

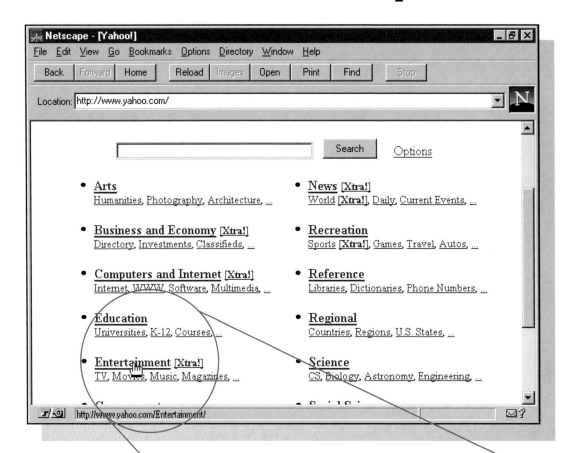

"Why would I do this?"

Yahoo has become something of a phenomenon on the Web. This is one of the most popular places on the Net to find other pages on the Web. Yahoo has a listing-type index with a wide variety of headings including a What's New, What's Cool, and What's Popular. Some of the more "traditional" subject headings include Art, Business, and Environment.

The other part of Yahoo is a search page that lets you search for a page based on what is in it.

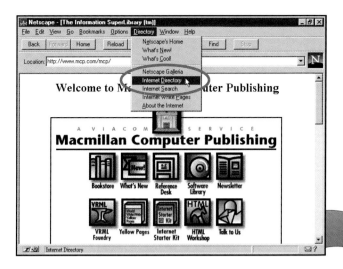

1 From any page in Netscape, open the **Directory** menu and choose the **Internet Directory** option.

TIP ▼

If you have the directory buttons bar visible, click the Net Directory button to open this page.

2 Scroll down the page and click on the **Yahoo** link.

TIP ▼

You can go directly to the Yahoo page by entering the address http://www.yahoo.com.

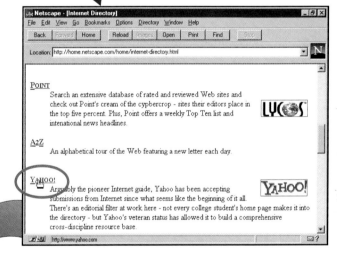

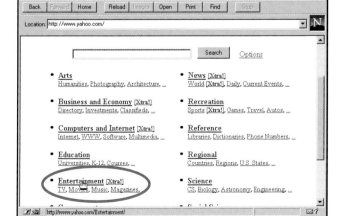

3 Click on any of the topic links that look interesting. In this task, I'm going to click the **Entertainment** link.

NOTE ▼

You can click one of the links from the list or any of the What's New, What's Cool, and other links under Yahoo.

4 This opens up another list of subcategories for Entertainment. Click on any of these links to see what is in these subtopics. Here, I'm jumping to the **COOL links** link.

NOTE ▼

You can jump back to the main Yahoo page from any of the Yahoo categories by clicking Yahoo, which is at the top of every page of the listings.

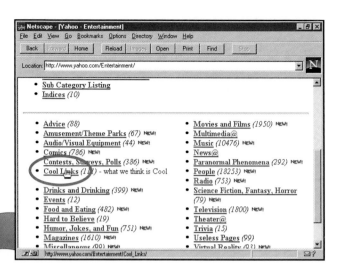

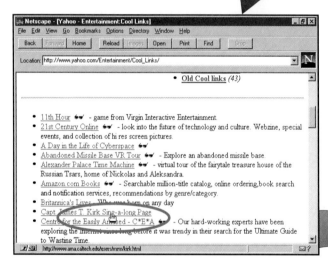

5 The COOL links link opens a list with links to several more categories but most of this page contains links to other individual pages. You can go another level deeper into the listings or click one of the page names to jump to a page like the Capt. James T. Kirk Sing-a-long page.

6 If you don't find a link that interests you by looking through the links, try scrolling back up to the top of one of the pages of the listing and click on the **Options** link next to the search button.

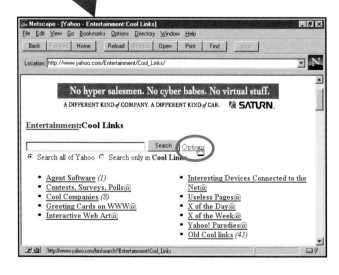

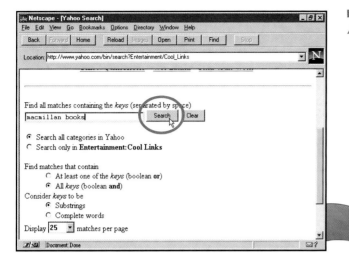

7 Enter the information you want to search for. This example will search for Macmillan and books. (Because the All *keys* (boolean **and**) option is selected, this will search for documents that contain both "Macmillan" and "books.") When you have entered the search, click the **Search** button.

8 The search returns a page with a list of all of the pages that match with links to each one. You can see here that this search found three matches.

TASK 16
Excite

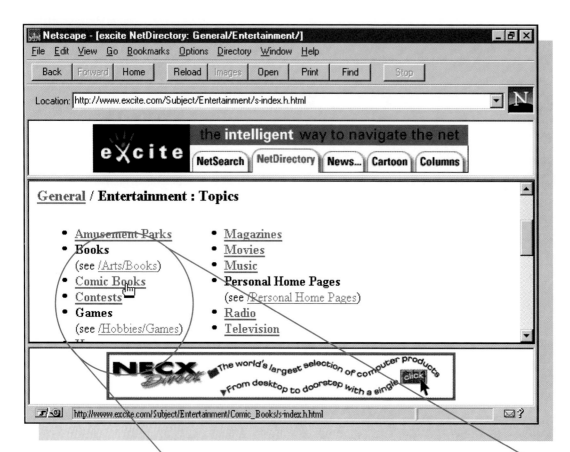

"Why would I do this?"

Excite is another combination of an index of listings and a search page like Yahoo. Excite is so popular, Netscape features it as their main directory at the Netscapte Directory page.

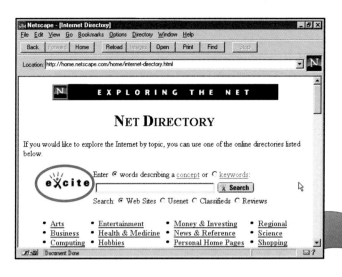

1 From any page in Netscape, open the Directory menu and choose the Interent Directory option. The Excite directory is at the top of the page.

2 From the list of topics below Excite, click any topic of interest.

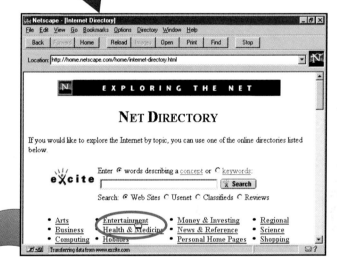

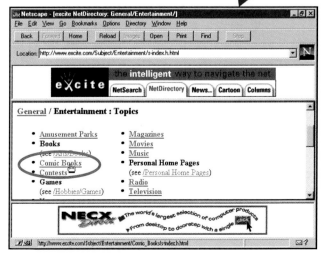

3 You can click on any of the headings to open a list of the subcategories.

4 Click on any of the links to go to any of the pages.

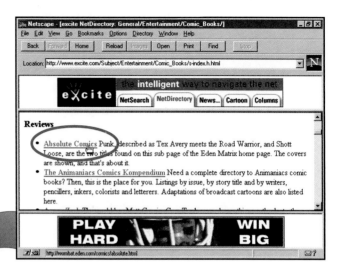

5 If you don't find a link you want to go to, click the NetSearch tab in the upper frame.

NOTE ▼

The three different horizontal sections of the Excite web page here are called *frames*. Frames are a new feature in Netscape 2 that allow web page designers to create multiple sections within a single Netscape screen that each have their own URL address. These can be linked together or totally independent. For more information on frames see http://home.netscape.com /comprod/products/navigator/version_ 2.0/index.html.

6 Enter the word to search for and click Search.

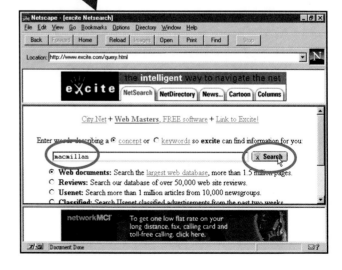

Internet Searches

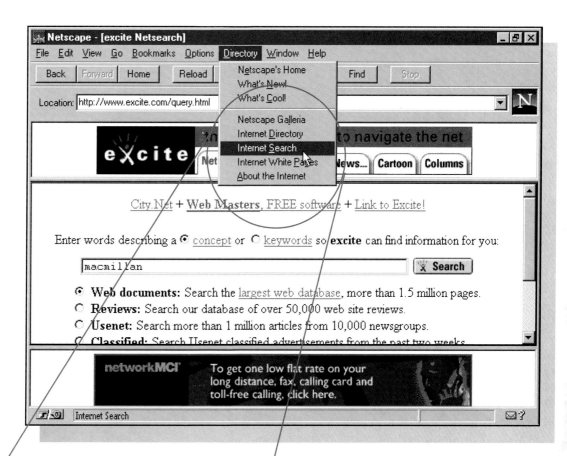

"Why would I do this?"

If you read the last two tasks, you may wonder why you would need a Web page that searches for other pages for you. After all, the Yahoo and Excite indexes have links to thousands of pages, more links than you'll ever follow. And they even have some basic searching features.

But what if you don't know where to look in the index? Star Trek pages are probably under Entertainment, but from there, should you look under TV or Movies? This task will introduce you to several Web search pages that help you find Web pages based on topic and content.

1 Netscape has built a page with links and descriptions for several of the most popular Web search pages. To open this page, open the **Directory** menu and choose the **Internet Search** option.

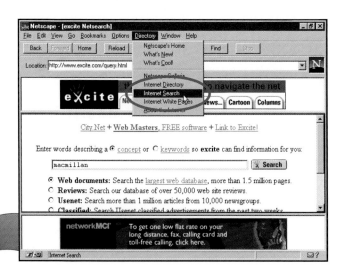

> **NOTE** ▼
>
> The URL address for this page is http://home.netscape.com/home/internet-search.html.

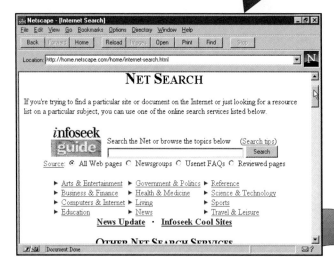

2 This opens the Internet Search page.

> **TIP** ▼
>
> If you have the directory buttons bar visible, click the Net Search button to open this page.

3 Scroll down through this page until you find the listings of Search Engines. Note that there is a link for each engine along with a description.

Clicking on any of these links will open one of the search pages. In Tasks 18 through 20, we'll look at several of the better ones.

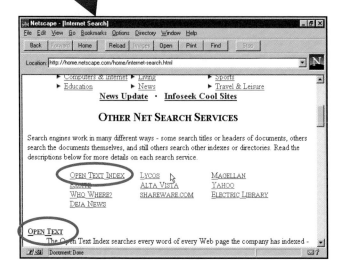

The Lycos Searcher

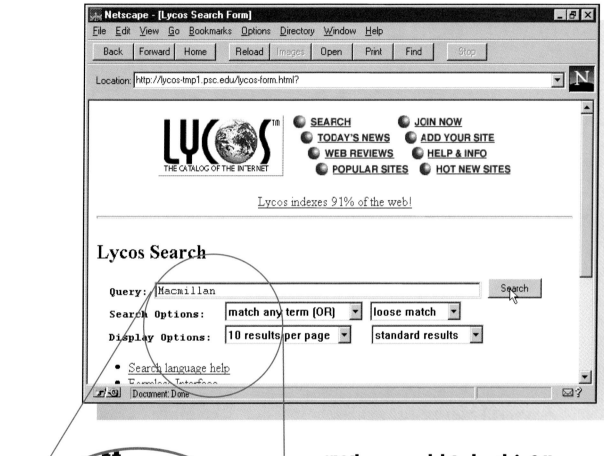

"Why would I do this?"

The Lycos search page boasts the biggest database of Web pages I've seen. As of this writing, they claim almost twenty million URL addresses have been indexed. They've been adding a million or so addresses to this index every month for a few months now. So, if you are looking to find every Web page that might be related to a topic, there's a good chance that they'll have them all in this index.

1 From the Internet Search page at the end of the last task, click the **Lycos** link. Or, you can enter the URL address **http://www.lycos.com**.

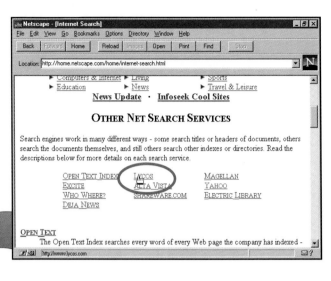

2 Click the **Search Options** link. This link gives you access to all of Lycos powerful search options.

3 In this form, enter what you want to look for in the Query box. The other boxes control how the search is performed. Display options determines how many matching pages will be listed on each page. This is 10 by default. If you type more than one word in the query, and want only pages that match more than one query term, select the number of words that need to match in the Search Options. When you are done, click the **Search** button.

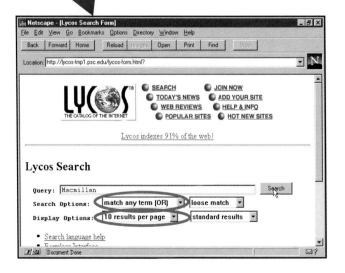

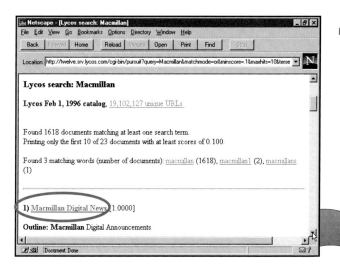

4 After a bit of a wait (depending on how busy the server is) you should get a page showing the results of the search. At the top of the page, it will tell you how many matches were found. Here, 1618 pages containing Macmillan were found. Below the line, there are links to the first 10 pages that match. With each match is a score, ranging from 0 to 1. Documents scoring a 1 are the best matches.

5 After looking at the results, scroll to the bottom of the page.

To narrow the search, type Que into the Refine Search box with Macmillan. Then click **Search**.

WHY WORRY?

If you get a message stating that the server is too busy, go back to the Lycos home page and try the search again later.

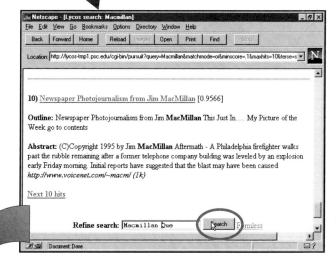

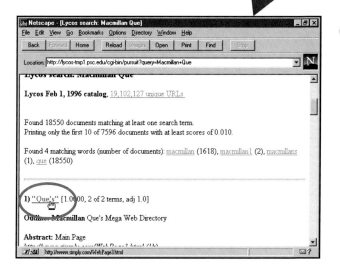

6 This time the results look a little different. While there were more matches overall, the ones with Macmillan and Que get the highest scores and are at the top of the list.

TASK 19

The WebCrawler

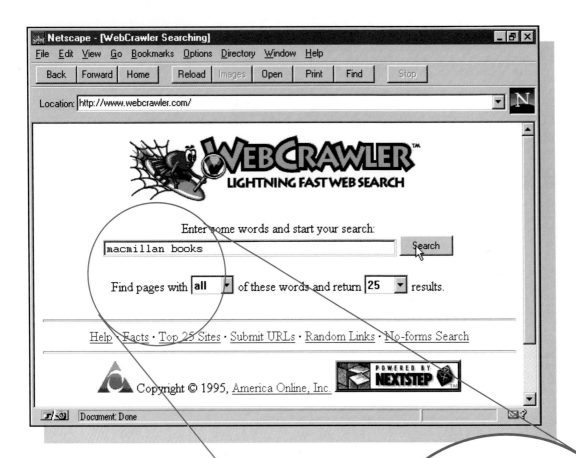

"Why would I do this?"

The WebCrawler was one of the first popular Web search pages. They must have a very good server for this because it is fast and rarely busy.

The downside for this search page is that it doesn't have as many pages in the database as Lycos. But you'll still find matches for most searches.

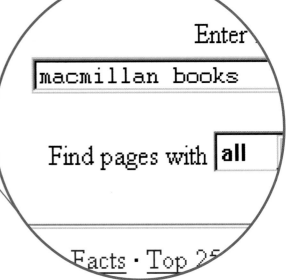

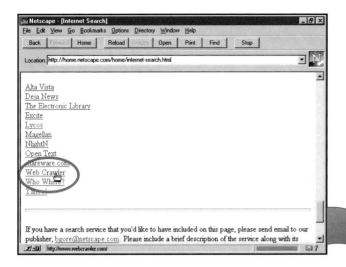

1 From the Internet search page (the end of Task 17), Click the link for WebCrawler. Or enter the URL address http://www.webvrawler.com.

NOTE ▼

How do the searchers "score" the pages? Without going into too much detail, the more times the search word is found in a document, the higher the score. If the term is found in the title of the document, it will get a high score. More points are also given for matches found near the beginning of the page. All of these factors are weighed to determine a score.

2 In the box, enter the words to search for. If you enter more than one word and only want pages that include all of the words, select the **all** option. To change the number of matches, select the box that has 25 in it and pick a different number from the list. When you are done, click **Search**.

3 The Search Results page will list all of the matching documents, up to the number you selected. The best matches are at the top. The highest score is 100. Click any of these links to go to the matching page.

TASK 20

Alta Vista

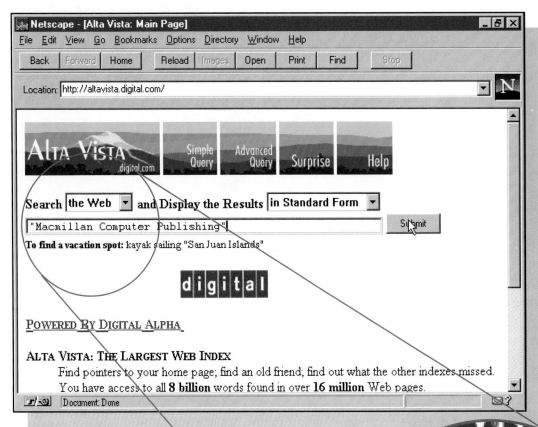

"Why would I do this?"

The last Web search page we are going to try is the Alta Vista page. This page has over 20 million pages indexed. Alta Vista keeps the pressure on Lycos to keep adding to their site, a healthy competition for users.

This page has about 16 million pages indexed. Alta Vista keeps the pressure on Lycos to keep adding to their index, a healthy competition for users.

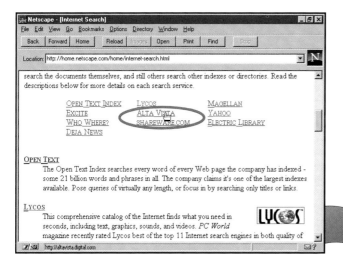

1 From the Internet Search page (the end of Task 17), click the link for Alta Vista. Or you can enter the URL address **http://altavista.digital.com**.

2 Enter the word to search for in the box. If you are search for a phrase enclose it in quotes.

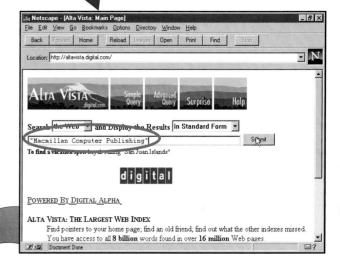

3 The best matches are listed first in the results, Here, a Macmillan Computer Publishing page is second from the top.

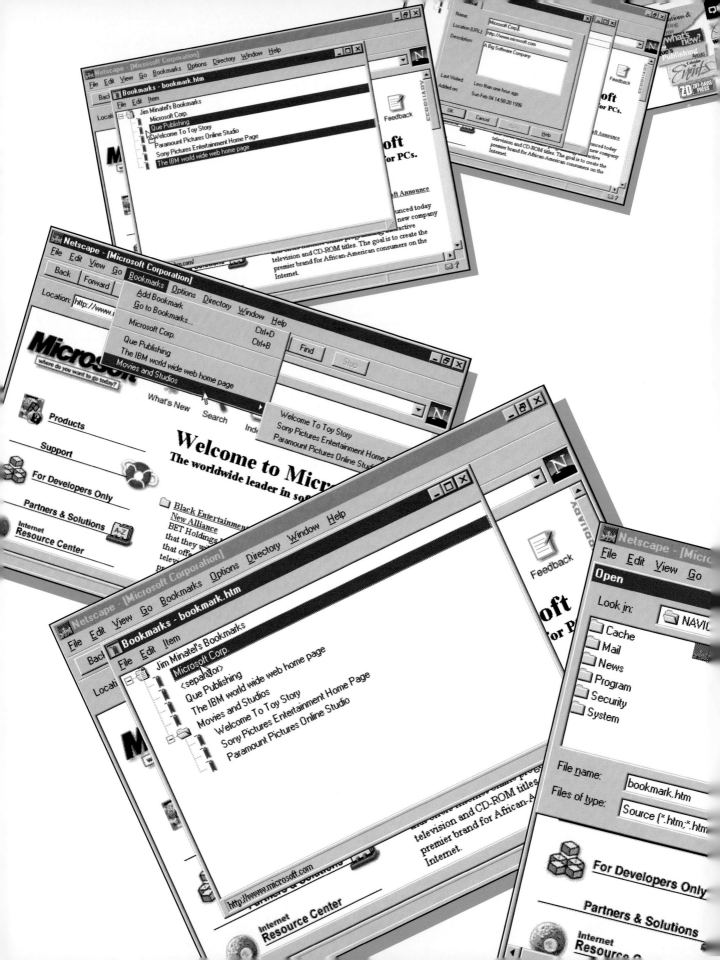

PART IV

Bookmarks: Shortcuts to Your Favorite Places

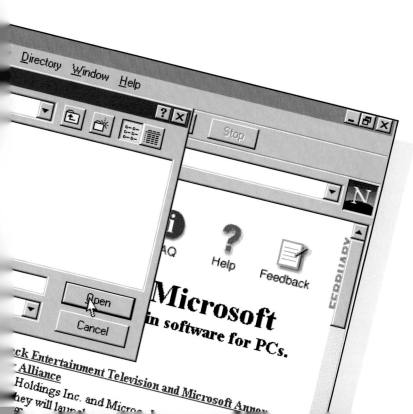

After you've been cruising the Web for a while, you will find that there are some favorite Web pages that you like to visit repeatedly. Maybe you often use the Macmillan Information SuperLibrary at **http://www.mcp.com** to keep informed about the latest computer books and events in the computer industry. Or maybe your favorite places are geared more toward fun like the United Federation of Planets site at **http://www.ufp.org**.

It's easy to make a mistake when you type in an address like this. And you need to keep all of these addresses handy unless you plan to memorize the addresses for your favorite places. The lure of the Web is that it makes getting to Internet documents easy, and there's nothing easy about memorizing addresses.

You can also get to these pages the same way you found them the first time. If you used the Yahoo directory to find the Star Trek pictures page, you can go back to the Yahoo directory and click Entertainment, then work your way through several sublevels until you find the Star Trek page again. But this wastes valuable time. Clicking through a series of links to open the one page you want can get tiresome quickly.

Netscape has devised a quick and easy way to help you get to these favorite pages any time you want without typing in the address or jumping through a long series of pages. This feature is called Bookmarks. A bookmark in Netscape works just like a bookmark in a book: You put a bookmark in a book so you can find your place in the book without flipping through page after page looking for where you left off.

A bookmark in Netscape saves the address of the marked page for you so that you don't have to type it in again to get to the page. The bookmark also saves the name of the page. This way you can save several bookmarks and jump to anything just by recognizing the name.

Unlike a traditional bookmark in a book, where you would usually just keep one bookmark to show where you finished, you can keep many bookmarks in Netscape. This is great because you can make a bookmark for each of your favorite pages.

But even this can become cumbersome. Netscape puts all of these bookmarks on a menu and if you get too many, you'll spend a lot of time scrolling through the menu looking for the bookmark you want. You can even get so many bookmarks that you can't see them all.

In Netscape, you have several options to control these bookmarks. You can create hierarchical submenus that branch off the main bookmark menu. This will save you space on the main menu and help you organize the bookmarks to find them easily. You might put all of your computer-book-related bookmarks in one submenu, science fiction series bookmarks in another, and government information in still a third. This way, when you need to find the latest press release from the White House (**http://www.whitehouse.gov**) you will know exactly where to find it on your bookmark list and you won't lose it among the Star Trek pages.

In this part, we'll show you bookmark basics such as adding a bookmark and jumping to it. These may be the only two bookmark features you ever need. But if you are interested in keeping your bookmark list neatly organized, you'll also learn how to make submenus, rearrange the order of bookmarks on the list, delete bookmarks that you never use, and even edit bookmarks so that you can recognize them more easily.

Adding a Bookmark and Jumping to a Bookmark

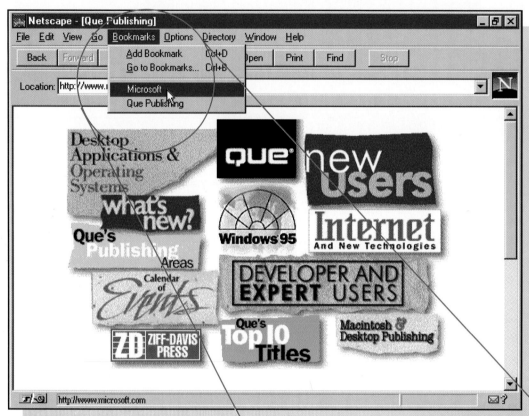

"Why would I do this?"

If you are viewing a page that you think you will come back to and want to make it easy to find, you should add a bookmark for it. You don't even need to be viewing a page to add a bookmark for it. If you know the address of a page, you can add a bookmark with the address.

Once you've added bookmarks, you'll use them by jumping to the pages that they link to.

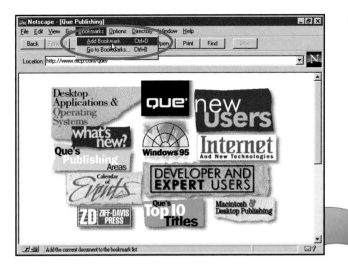

1 If you are viewing a page that you want to add a bookmark for, open the **Bookmarks** menu and choose the **Add Bookmark** option.

TIP ▼

You can also add a bookmark for a link on the current page by clicking anywhere on the link with the right mouse button and choosing Add Bookmark for this link from the popup menu.

2 If you open the **Bookmarks** menu now, you will see that a new menu option has been added at the bottom of the menu. This is the bookmark that you added.

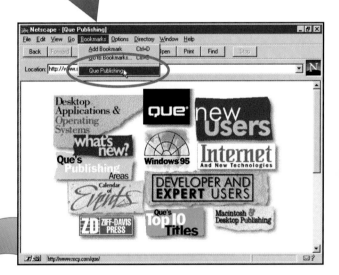

3 If you have an URL address for a Web page that you want to add a bookmark for, open the **Bookmarks** menu and choose the **Go to Bookmarks** option.

4 In the bookmarks Window, open the Item menu and choose the Insert Bookmark option.

> **TIP**
>
> You can open a page from a bookmark in the dialog box any time the dialog box is open. To open a page, double click the bookmark in the list.

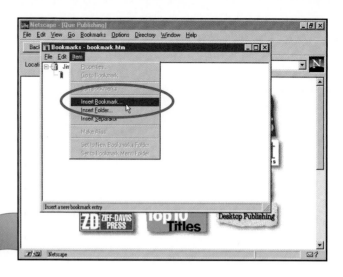

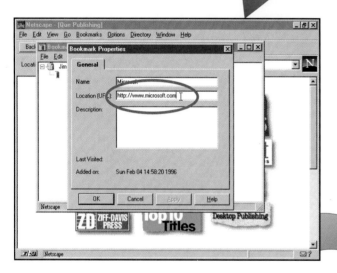

5 Enter the name of the page as you want it to appear in the bookmark list in the Name box. This can be the real name from the page, or it can be a name that is easy for you to recognize.

Enter the URL address of the page in the Location box. Be sure to enter the exact address.

6 After you have entered this, click the **OK** button.

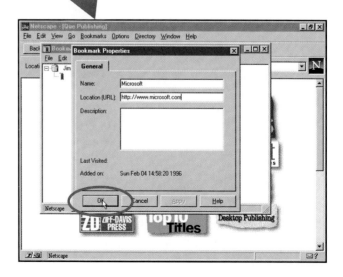

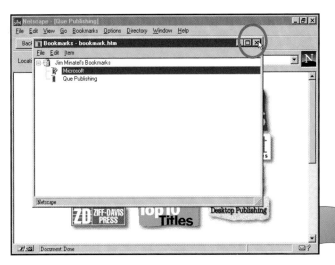

7 The page you added is now added to the list. Click the window close button (the X in the upper right corner).

8 Now open the **Bookmarks** menu. The bookmark that you added in the dialog box is now added to the bookmark list. Open the page for any of the bookmarks you have added by selecting it from the menu.

> **NOTE** ▼
>
> If you don't like the order the bookmarks appear in the menu, see Task 23 to see how to rearrange the list.

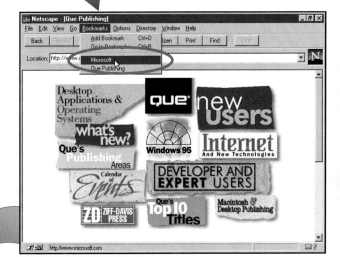

9 After selecting the bookmark from the menu, the page for that bookmark will open. You can also add a bookmark by clicking the right mouse button on a link on a Web page and choosing the Add Bookmark for this Link option from the pop-up menu.

Editing a Bookmark

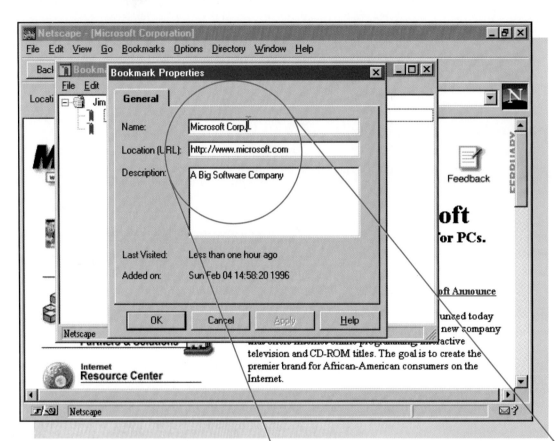

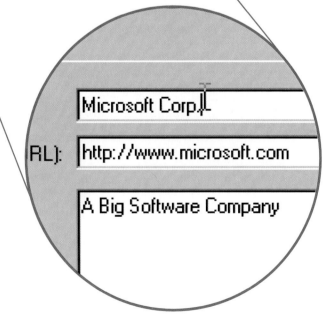

"Why would I do this?"

When you add a bookmark for a page you are viewing, Netscape automatically gives the bookmarks the same name as the page. Sometimes the name of the page might not always be the best way for you to recognize it. You may want to give the bookmark a name that is easier for you to recognize. You'll also need to edit a bookmark when the address for the page changes. Just as people and businesses move and change their addresses, Web pages sometimes move. When this happens, your old bookmarks won't work anymore and you will need to change the addresses.

1 To edit a bookmark, open the **Bookmarks** menu and choose **Go to Bookmarks**.

2 Select the bookmark that you want to edit by clicking on it in the list. Then click on it with the right muse button and choose properties form the pop-up menu.

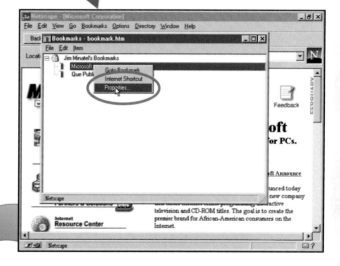

3 Make any changes you want to the name of the bookmark in the Name box. If the address has changed, enter the correct new address in the Location box.

If you want to add some more descriptive information about the bookmark, type a description in the Description box. When you are done making your changes, click the **OK** button.

TASK 23

Rearranging the Bookmark List

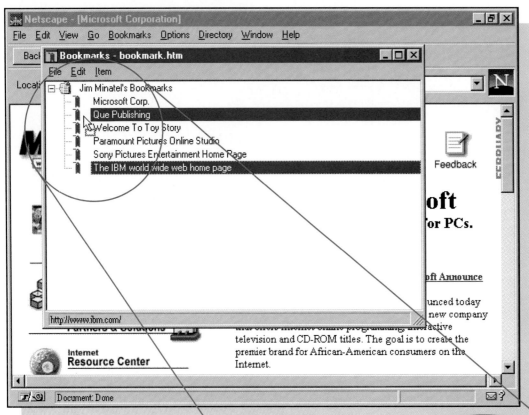

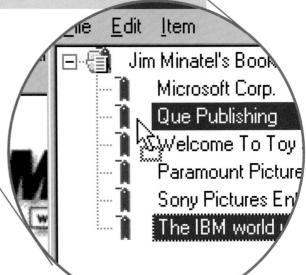

"Why would I do this?"

When you add bookmarks, they are added to the bottom of the list in the order you add them. It's easy to create a bookmark list with all of your bookmarks mixed up in no particular order.

If you want to group the bookmarks in your list so that entries that are related to each other are close to each other on the list, use Netscape to rearrange the list.

1 To rearrange the bookmarks in your bookmark list, open the **Bookmarks** menu and choose the **Go to Bookmarks** option.

2 Select a bookmark that you want to move by clicking on it in the list. Move it up or down in the list by dragging it, just like you click, drag, and drop in a word processor.

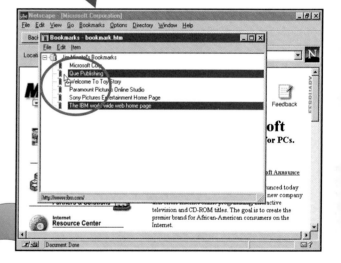

3 When you drag an item, the bookmark above where the moved bookmark will appear is highlighted. Here, the highlighted bookmark in step 2 was Que Publishing. The IBM Bookmark is moved below it.

Adding Submenus and Separators to the Bookmark List

"Why would I do this?"

When you have a lot of bookmarks, you may want to make the list shorter without deleting items. You can group some related bookmarks together by adding a header, which is what Netscape uses to group bookmarks into submenus. When the bookmark menu has a submenu, there will be a small triangle pointing to the right next to it in the menu. You can also add separators, which are horizontal lines in the menu that visually divide the menu.

1 To add headers or When the bookmark menu has a submenu, there will be a small triangle pointing tseparators to the

bookmark menu, open the **Bookmarks** menu and choose **Go to Bookmarks**.

2 Select the bookmark above where you want to add a separator by clicking the

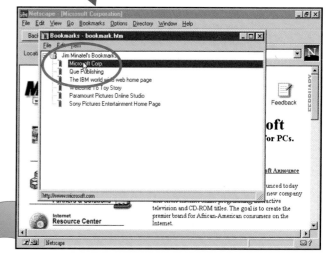

bookmark.

3 In the Bookmark window, open the Item menu and choose the Insert Separator option.

4 To create a submenu, select the bookmark above where you want the new heading to appear. Open the Item menu and choose the Insert Folder option.

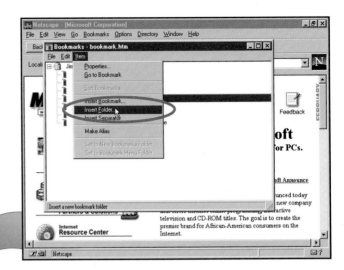

5 Enter a name for the new submenu in the Name box. This name can be anything you want to call it. Leave the other boxes blank. Then click OK.

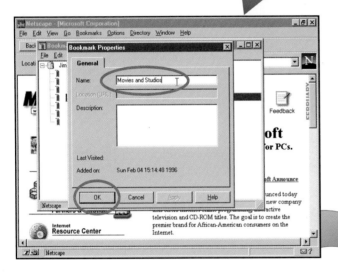

6 To arrange the bookmarks so that they appear as part of the submenu, select a bookmark and drag it to the folder for the submenu. Repeat this step for all of the bookmarks that you want to make part of the submenu. When you are done, click the window close button. When you open the bookmark menu, you should see the header with the triangle to the right. Select this item and your submenu will open.

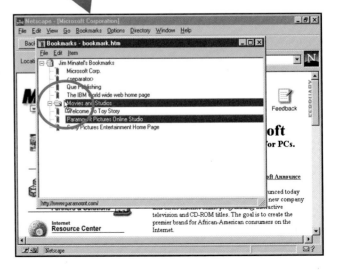

Removing a Bookmark

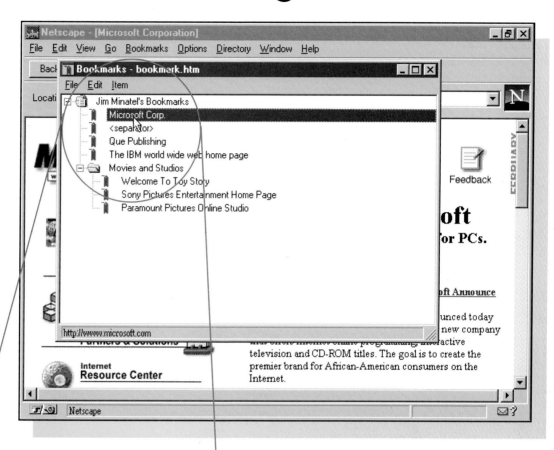

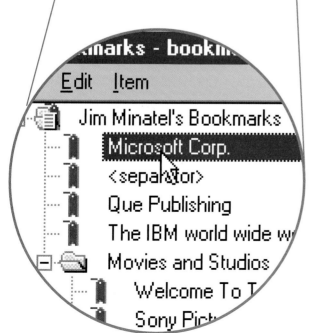

"Why would I do this?"

It's so easy to add bookmarks in Netscape that you may be tempted to add bookmarks for every good Web site that you see. But you'll soon find that you have more bookmarks than you can use. So it's helpful to be able to delete bookmarks that you are less interested in or don't use anymore.

1 Open the **Bookmarks** menu and choose **Go to Bookmarks**.

2 Select the bookmark that you want to delete in the list of bookmarks by clicking it. Then press the delete key.

3 The next time you open the **Bookmarks** menu, you will see that the item you removed is gone from the list.

Viewing Your Bookmarks as a Web Page

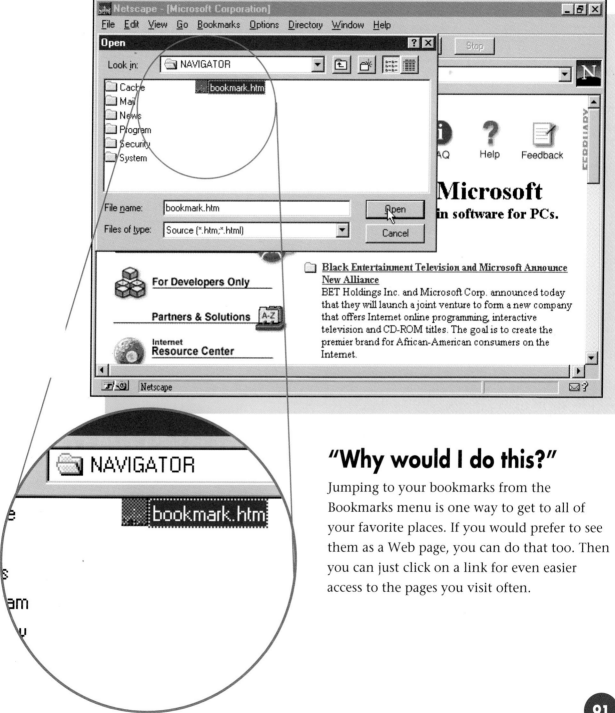

"Why would I do this?"

Jumping to your bookmarks from the Bookmarks menu is one way to get to all of your favorite places. If you would prefer to see them as a Web page, you can do that too. Then you can just click on a link for even easier access to the pages you visit often.

1 Open the **File** menu and choose the **View Open File** option.

2 Change directories to the c:\Program Files\NETSCAPE \NAVIGATOR directory and choose the bookmark .htm file. Then click Open.

WHY WORRY?

If you installed Netscape in a directory other than the default in Task 3, look there for the bookmark file.

3 Your bookmarks are now displayed as a Web page. Click on any of these links to jump to one of these pages.

NOTE ▼

If you want to make your bookmarks into your home page, so that this bookmark page is the first thing you see when you start Netscape or click Home, follow the steps in Task 10 to change your home page. For the address, enter the same address that is in the location bar in step 3.

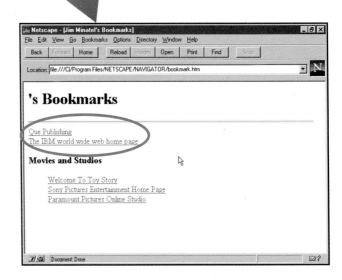

Jumping to a Page
in the History List

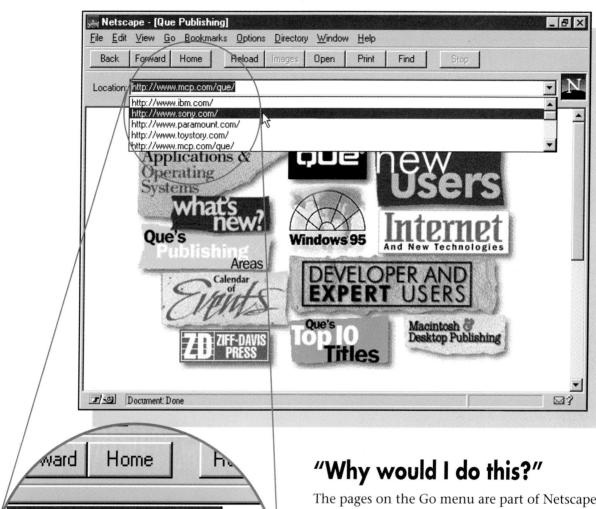

"Why would I do this?"

The pages on the Go menu are part of Netscape's history list, which tracks all of the pages that you visit so you can jump back to them at any time.

The list at the bottom of the Go menu is limited to 15 entries. The History list keeps track of all of the pages you go to.

1 Click the arrow at the right of the location bar.

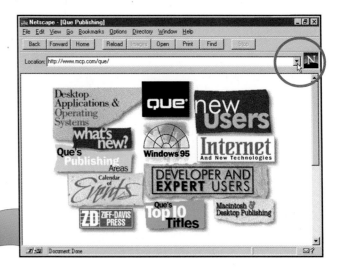

2 Scroll through the Histroy list and select the page you want to view by clicking it.

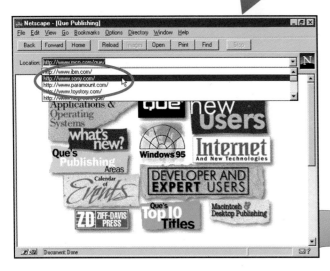

3 This opens the page that you selected.

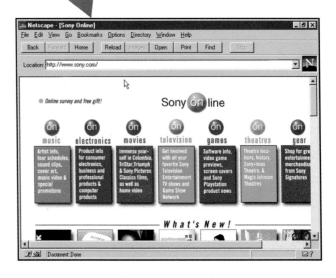

Checking For Changed Bookmark Links

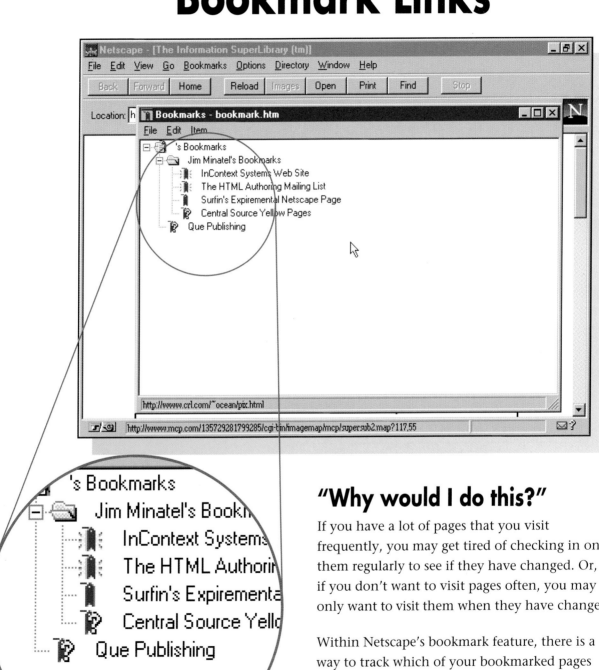

"Why would I do this?"

If you have a lot of pages that you visit
frequently, you may get tired of checking in on
them regularly to see if they have changed. Or,
if you don't want to visit pages often, you may
only want to visit them when they have changed.

Within Netscape's bookmark feature, there is a
way to track which of your bookmarked pages
have changed since you last loaded the page.
When you run this feature, Netscape will mark
the changed pages with a different icon in the
bookmark window. Then you will know
which pages have changed.

1 If you want to check just some of your bookmarks for changes in the pages, select those in the Bookmarks window by clicking on them. (Hold the Ctrl key while clicking to select more than one.) Then open the File menu and choose the What's New Option.

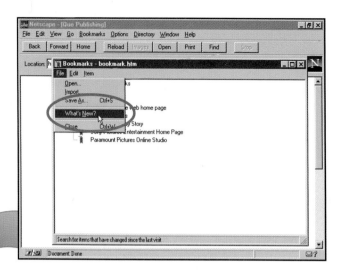

2 Select whether to check just selected bookmarks or all of your bookmarks for changes. (Checking all bookmarks could take a while.) Then click Start Checking.

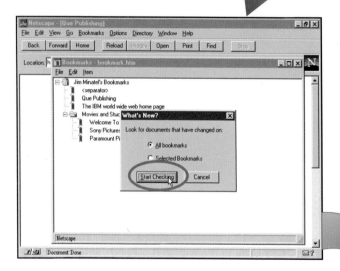

TIP ▼

While the pages are being checked, Netscape displays a dialog showing its progress. Netscape is connecting to each site automatically and checking for changes. Netscape displays an estimate of the time remaining and gives you a Cancel option to stop the process if you decide it is taking too long.

3 When the check is complete, you will see a dialog box telling you how many web pages (documents) from your bookmarks list have changed since you last visited them. Click OK.

In the Bookmarks window, the icon next to the changed bookmarks will change. They will have little lines next to them like the InContext Systems and HTML Authoring Mailing Lists bookmarks on page 95. The question marks show that Netscape cannot tell if those pages have changed.

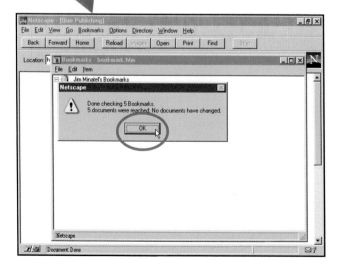

Speeding Up Your Favorite Pages

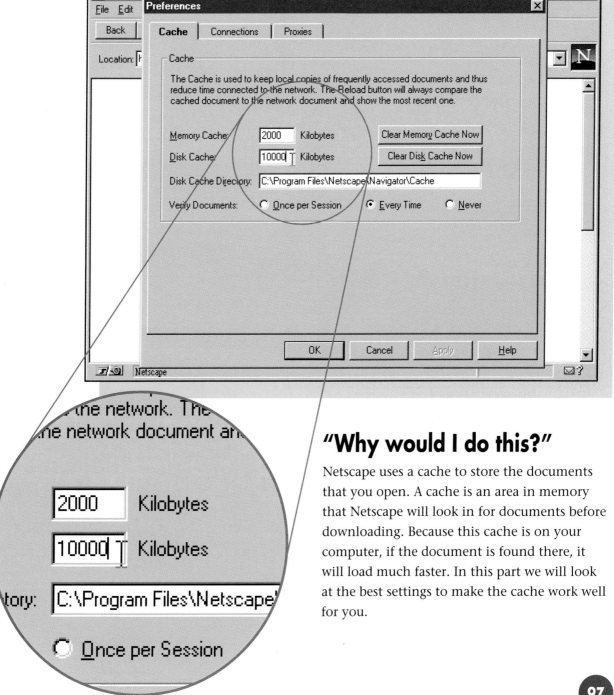

"Why would I do this?"

Netscape uses a cache to store the documents that you open. A cache is an area in memory that Netscape will look in for documents before downloading. Because this cache is on your computer, if the document is found there, it will load much faster. In this part we will look at the best settings to make the cache work well for you.

1 Open the **Options** menu and choose **Preferences**.

2 At the top of the dialog box, click on the down arrow and select **Cache and Network** from the list.

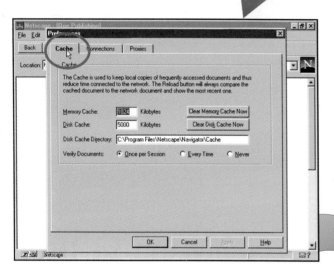

TIP

If the pages that you load don't change very often, you can set Verify Documents to Once per Session or never to save a little time as described in step 3.

3 Once a document is in your cache, it stays the same, even if the Web page changes. When you open a page in Netscape that you have loaded before, Netscape checks the beginning of the page on the Web each time you load the page. If it is the same, it loads the rest of the document from your cache to save time. If it's different, it loads the changed version from the Web.

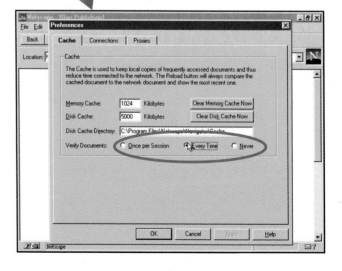

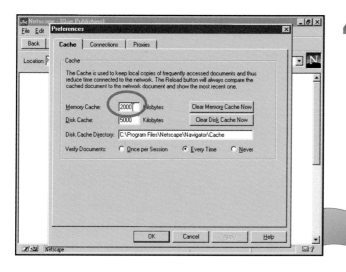

4 Netscape's cache is divided into two parts. The memory cache is used for the most recently used documents and is stored in RAM. This is the fastest part of the cache. If you have a computer with 8 or 16Mb of RAM and you don't run many other applications while you are running Netscape, you can change this setting from 600 to 1000 or 2000. The higher you set this, the more documents will be saved in RAM and the faster they will load.

5 The other part of the cache is the disk cache. The disk cache can be much larger than the memory cache and it is also more permanent. It is saved even when you exit Netscape and turn off the computer. But it is slower than the memory cache. (It is still *much* faster than downloading a page from the Web.) So, if you have a large hard drive with a lot of free space, you may want to increase this number from 5000 to 10000.

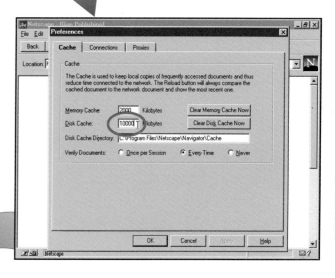

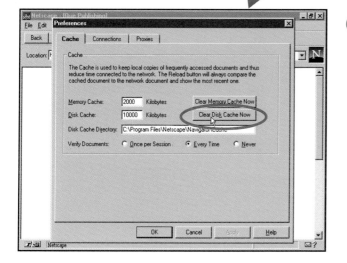

6 When your memory cache or disk cache gets full, Netscape makes room for new files by deleting the oldest ones. When the disk cache gets full, Netscape slows down. At this point, you can increase the size of the cache or clear the cache. Clearing the cache will make more room for new documents to load quickly. But anything that was already in the cache will have to be reloaded. To clear the Disk Cache, click the **Clear Disk Cache Now** button.

7 Netscape will show you a dialog box warning you that clearing the cache will mean any pages in it need to be reloaded from the Web the next time you open them. If you want to do this, click **OK**.

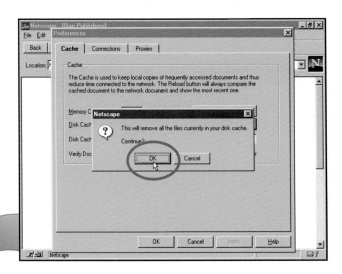

NOTE ▼

If you have opened a lot of pages that you don't think you will ever look at again, clearing the disk cache may be a good idea. If you generally load the same pages on a regular basis and these pages don't change, clearing the cache is probably not a good idea.

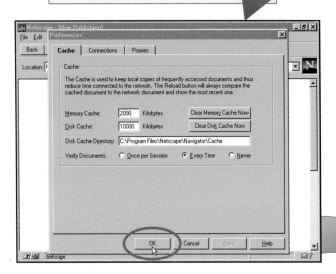

8 When you've made all of the changes you want to in the cache settings, click **OK**.

9 Open the **Options** menu and choose **Save Options** to save your changes to the cache settings.

WHY WORRY?

If you think that Netscape is loading a page of the cache that may have changed, click the Reload button to load a fresh copy from the Web site. Netscape should do this correctly without you having to click the Reload button, but in some cases it doesn't.

PART V
Experiencing Multimedia

In this part, we'll take a look at multimedia on the Web. What is multimedia? Multimedia is the combination of text, picture, sound, and even movies and even interactive games. We'll look at how to find multimedia files on the Web and what to do with them once you've found them.

The simplest and most popular type of multimedia file on the Web is a picture. One of the most popular picture sites is a NASA page that has images of 1994's collision of a comet with Jupiter (**http://newproducts.jpl.nasa.gov /sl9/sl9.html**). Other popular pages include Doctor Fun, which is a cartoon you can download (**http://www.Unitedmedia.com/ comics/drfun**) and pictures from movies produced by Paramount (**http://www.paramount.com**). The variety is endless.

Netscape can download and display pictures just like any other Web page. For the two most common types of pictures on the Web—GIF and JPEG—Netscape downloads the files without any additional work.

The next type of multimedia file we'll explore is sound. You can find sounds from sources as diverse as David Letterman (**http://bingen.cs.csbsju.edu /letterman/lswdl_sounds.html**) and President Clinton (**http://www.whitehouse.gov**).

Netscape includes an audio player for listening to sounds. The most common format you will find for sounds is AU, which the Netscape player plays. In addition to this, you will need a sound card (properly installed and configured) and speakers or headphones. We'll also show you how to configure Netscape to use Windows Media Player to play .wav files.

A new feature in Netscape 2 is called a Plug-in. Plug-ins are used to let you work with different types of files directly within Netscape, without opening a separate application. For example, there are plug-ins available that allow you to work with spreadsheets in Netscape, edit and manipulate graphics, and view pages laid out with programs like Adobe Acrobat. The plug-in we'll look at in some detail is Macromedia's Shockwave. Shockwave allows web page designers to incorporate animation and interactivity into their web sites. This can be used in a variety of ways. In some sites it is used just to add a bit of pizzazz, others use it for enhanced navigation, and some even use it to deliver web based games.

If you find yourself using a lot of multimedia files, there are several helper applications and plug-ins you may need. These applications are used to view movies, open Zip files, and other things Netscape can't do. Here is a short list of helper applications, the types of files you use them for and where to find them:

File Type	File Extension	Where to Get Helper or Plug-In
QuickTime Movies	.mov	http://quicktime.apple.com/ form-qt2win.html
Zip Archives	.zip	http://www.winzip.com
AVI Movies	.avi	Use Windows Media Player
MPEG Movies	.pdf	http://www.adobe.com/Amber /Download.html

The QuickTime player, WinZip, and Media Player are used as helper applications. After installing these (Media Player is already installed by Windows), you'll configure Netscape to use them following the same general procedure outlined in Task 36.

The MPEG player and Acrobat viewer are both plug-ins. When you install these, they will automatically configure Netscape to open the proper type of file.

All of these applications include some directions for installing them at their download pages. After reading through the similar procedure in the book, installing any type of helper application or plug-in should be easy if you read the directions that come with it.

Netscape keeps a list of available Plug-ins at http://home.netscape.com/comprod/products/navigator/ version_2.0/plugins/index.html. You may want to check there occasionally to see if there are new plug-ins that you want to try.

TASK 30

Recognizing Multimedia Links

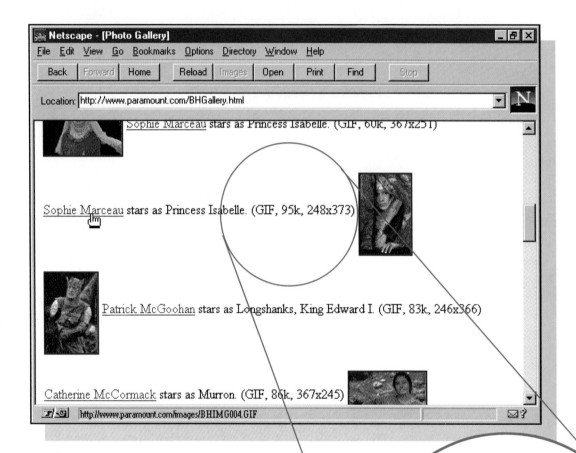

"Why would I do this?"

So you've heard all about how you can find great multimedia stuff on the Web. But how do you find pictures, movies, and sounds? And how can you tell what type of multimedia you have found before you download it?

This task will show you how to recognize a link to a multimedia file and how to know whether it is a picture, sound, or movie so you can decide if you want to download it.

1 We're going to look at the Braveheart page as one example to learn about different types of multimedia. The address for this page is **http://www.paramount.com/ BHGallery.html**.

> **NOTE** ▼
>
> If you need a refresher on opening a page with the URL address, see Task 6.

2 Scroll down the page and put the mouse pointer over the **Sophie Marceau** link. In the status bar, the file-name in the address ends with .GIF This extension is used to indicate a file that is a GIF picture. The other common extension you will see for pictures is .JPG. Some Web sites have begun to include information about the files in the page itself, as is the case here. After the link, the file type and size is given.

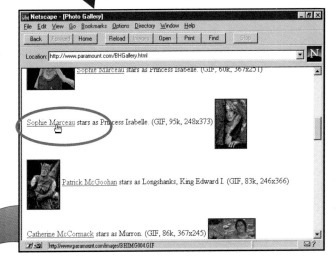

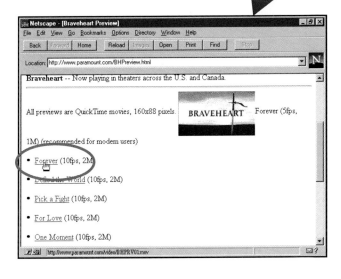

3 Now open the page at **http://www.paramount.com /BHPreview.html**. Move your mouse pointer to the link just a few lines up that reads **Forever**. In the The addressstatus bar, the file-name in the address ends with .mov. This extension is used to indicate a file that is a QuickTime movie. The other common movie extension is .MPG or .MPEG.

TASK 31

Viewing and Saving Pictures

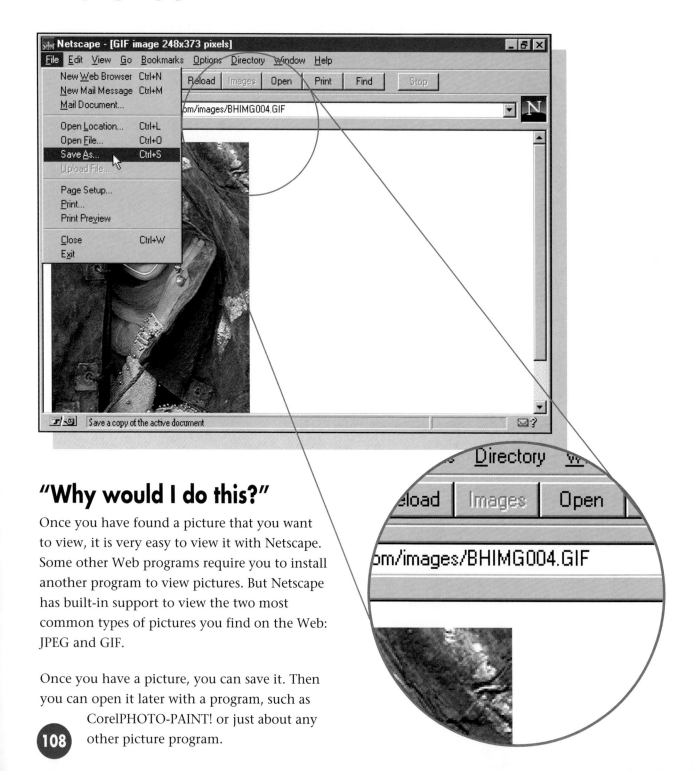

"Why would I do this?"

Once you have found a picture that you want to view, it is very easy to view it with Netscape. Some other Web programs require you to install another program to view pictures. But Netscape has built-in support to view the two most common types of pictures you find on the Web: JPEG and GIF.

Once you have a picture, you can save it. Then you can open it later with a program, such as CorelPHOTO-PAINT! or just about any other picture program.

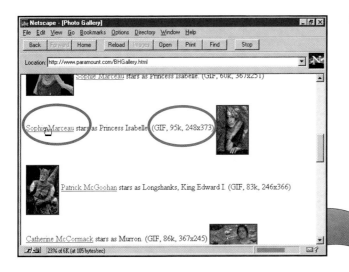

1 Open the URL **http://www. paramount.com/BHGallery.html**. Scroll down the page to the **Sophie Marceau** link. Notice when you put the mouse pointer on this link, the address ends with .GIF. As the text after the link states, this is a GIF picture, the file size is 95K and the picture will measure 248 pixels wide by 373 tall. When you are ready, click this link.

2 It should take roughly two minutes for this page to load if you are using a 14.4 modem. This will vary depending on the load on the server. Once the picture finishes downloading, Netscape will display it.

WHY WORRY?

If the picture looks grainy or the colors seem all wrong, you may need to select a 256-color video driver in Windows. If you don't know how to do this, you'll need to ask the tech support people where you got your computer how this is done.

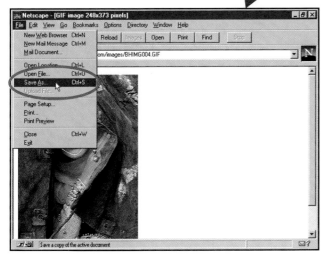

3 If you want to save the picture for later use with another program, open the **File** menu and choose the **Save as** option.

4 In the Save As dialog box, choose a drive and directory to save the file to. You will probably want to use the filename the picture had when you downloaded it. When you have selected a location, click **Save**.

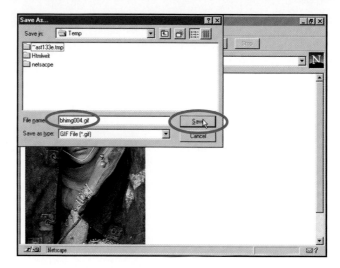

TASK 32
Listening to Sounds

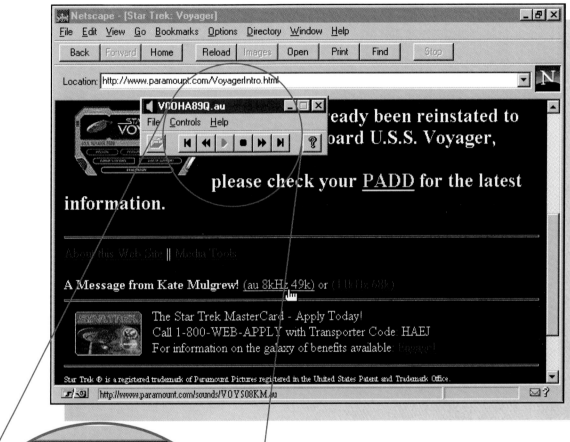

"Why would I do this?"

The Web isn't limited to just text and pictures. Sound files are another very popular type of multimedia on the Web. Even the President and Vice President have sound files on the Web. (You can find these at **http://www.whitehouse.gov**.)

To listen to sounds, you need to have a working sound card properly installed in your computer and speakers or headphones attached to it. (The sound quality on the internal speaker is so bad that it isn't worth the time it takes to download.)

1 For an example of an audio file, open the Star Trek page at **http://www. paramount.com/VoyagerIntro.html**. Scroll down the page until you find the **A Message from Kate Mulgrew** link. There are two links there, both to the same message but stored with slightly different quality. The first one is smaller and will download quicker and you won't notice much difference in quality between it and the other link. Click this link to begin the download.

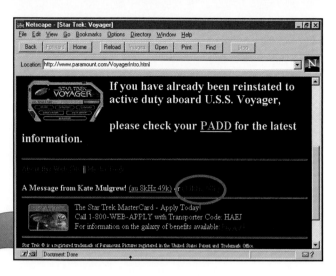

2 Once the file downloads, it will start Netscape's audio player and begin playing immediately. This player has a standard set of tape recorder controls for pausing, fast forwarding, and so on.

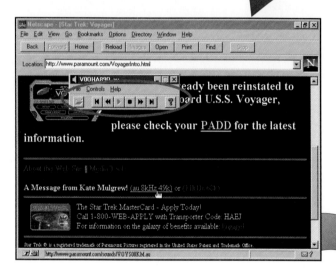

WHY WORRY?

Two features that are missing from this audio player are volume control and saving. If you want to change the volume, you'll have to use controls on the sound card or your speakers. To see how to save a sound, see Task 37.

3 To pause the sound, click the square button near the center of the controls. To continue playing, click the play button, which is the triangle facing right.

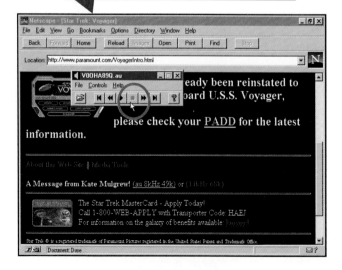

Getting the
Shockwave Plug-in

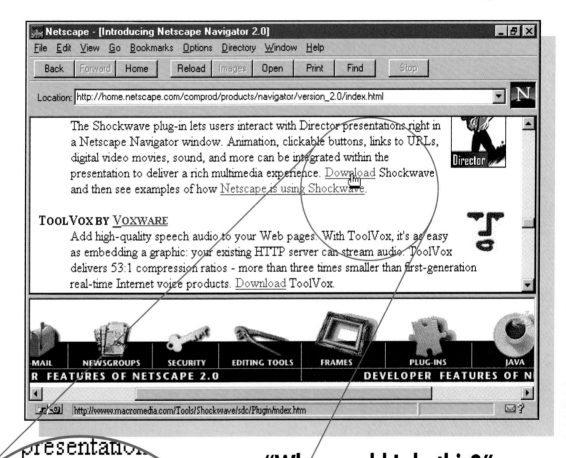

"Why would I do this?"

Macromedia has made their new Shockwave Plug-in available for free on the Web. Once you get and install the plug-in, you will be able to interact with Shockwave plug-in applications on the web. These can include games, animations, and anything else that makes use of movies, audio, and user interaction.

1 The first thing you need to do is create a temporary directory to save the file that you are about to download. Use Windows Explorer (or File Manager in Windows 3.1) to create this directory and name it \plugtemp.

Then, open the Web page at **http://home.netscape.com/ comprod/products/navigator /version_2.0/index.html**. Click the PLUG-INS link in the frame at the bottom of the page.

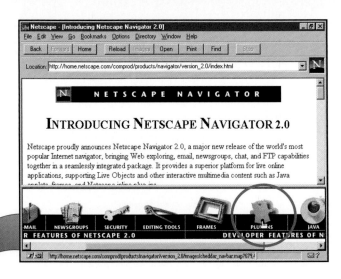

2 This opens the list at Netscape where they track all of the current plug-ins.

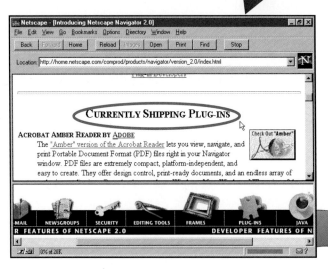

3 Scroll down through this page and find the entry for Macromedia Shockwave. Click the **Download** link.

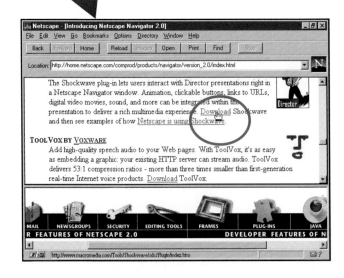

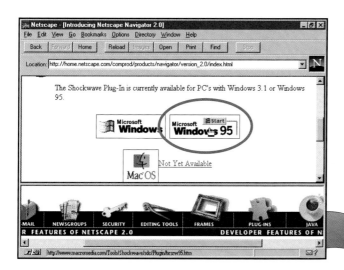

4 At the Shockwave page that opens, scroll down and click the link for Windows 95 (if that is the system you are using) or click the Windows link (for Windows 3.1 users).

5 Before you can download, Macromedia wants you to check to be sure you have Netscape 2. Since we know you have it, scroll down and click the **I've got the latest Netscape Navigator 2.0. Lets continue** link.

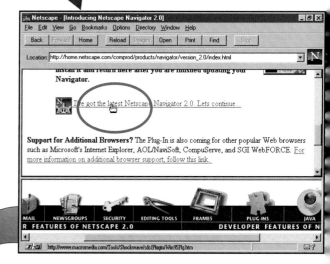

6 Scroll down to the list of places to get Shockwave. (Macromedia runs several FTP servers to provide support for more users to connect at once.) Click any one of these links, to download Shockwave.

7 After Netscape connects to the Shockwave site, the Save As dialog box will open. Change to the root directory of your hard drive and double click the plugtemp directory.

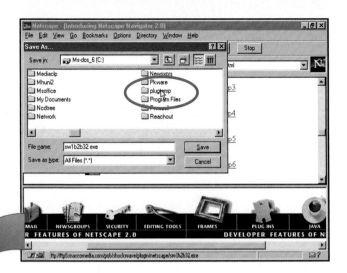

WHY WORRY?

If you get an error message that you can't connect instead of the Save As dialog, the Shockwave site is probably just busy. Try clicking one of the other FTP links from the Shockwave page or trying waiting and trying again later.

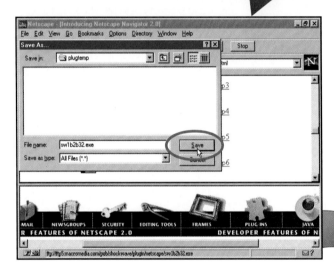

8 Click the **Save** button.

9 Netscape will now begin downloading the file. Netscape displays a dialog box showing the progress of the download and the remaining time. This should take about 8 - 10 minutes with a 28.8 modem.

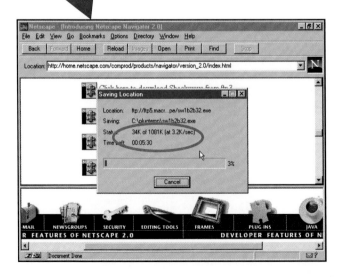

Installing Shockwave

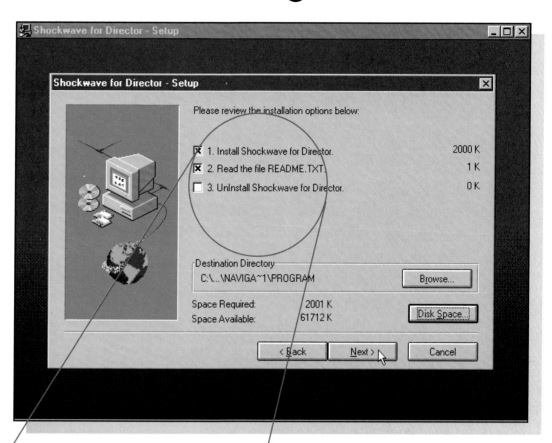

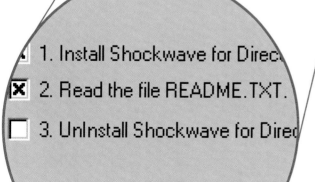

"Why would I do this?"

When you install Shockwave, the installer automatically configures Netscape to use it to open Shockwave pages on the web. After installation, whenever you open a page with a Shockwave application, Shockwave will automatically start in Netscape, and the application will be there for you.

1 Click on the **Start** menu to open it and choose the **Run** option.

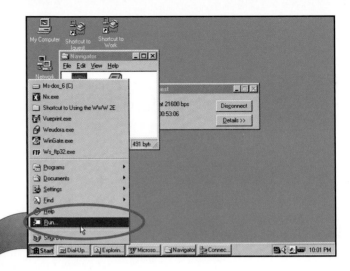

TIP ▼

To do this in Windows 3.1, open Program Manager's **File** menu and choose the **Run** option. The file names throughout this procedure and dialog boxes will be a little different for 3.1 users too.

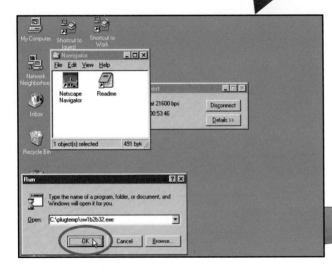

2 In the Open box, enter **c:\plugtemp \sw1b2b32.exe** and click **OK**.

WHY WORRY?

When you downloaded Shockwave, there may have been a newer version. Check the name of the file you downloaded and enter that here instead if it is different.

3 This will extract all of the files you need to install Shockwave. Watch the title in the DOS window that opens. When the title bar changes to "Finished," click the close window button (the X in the upper right) to close the Window.

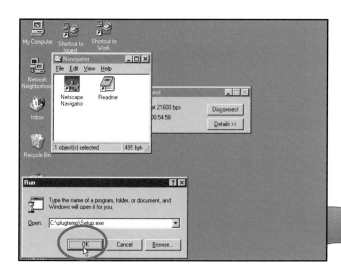

4 Click on the **Start** menu to open it and choose the **Run** option. This time, enter **c:\plugtemp\Setup.exe** in the Open box and click **OK**.

5 When you see the welcome screen for the Shockwave installer, click **Next**.

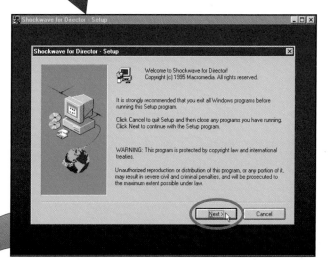

6 Be sure that the option for installing Shockwave is selected. Check the destination directory. Shockwave needs to be installed to the same directory as Netscape. In most cases, Shockwave finds this directory just fine on its own and you don't need to change anything. Then click **Next**.

7 The next thing you see is a dialog box showing the progress of the installer.

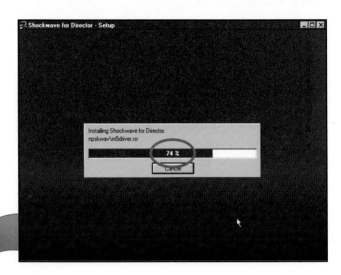

8 If the option to show the readme.txt file was selected in step 6, you'll now see Shockwave's updated notes. When you finish reading it, close Notepad.

9 After that, the installation will be complete. Click the **OK** button in this final dialog box to finish.

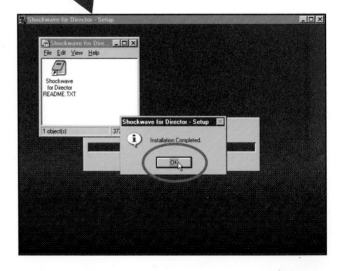

TASK 35
Playing Shockwave Pages

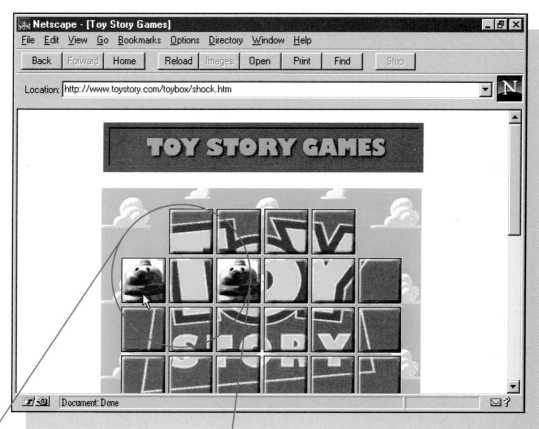

"Why would I do this?"

Once you have installed Shockwave, you are ready to use Netscape to explore some Shockwave pages. Netscape will start Shockwave when it needs to, without any prompting from you.

We'll look at an example of an interactive game with Shockwave in this task. If you want to see more Shockwave examples, check out Macromedia's list at http://www.macromedia.com/Tools/Shockwave/Gallery/index.html.

1 Open the web page http://www.toystory.
com/toybox/shock.htm.

As this page loads, a Macromedia
background will show up in the middle of
the screen. This is just a placeholder.
When the Shockwave application is
finished loading, the background will be
replaced by the application.

2 This is a game of "Concentration" based
on the "Toy Story" movie. To play, click
on the boxes to look for matches. You
click two boxes for each play. When you
get two pictures that match, the spaces
under them are uncovered. If they don't
match, the spaces are covered back up.

3 Here you see a square after it is clicked on.
All of the Shockwave application is
downloaded when you first download the
page so there is no waiting for pictures to
load when you click. If you have a sound
card and speakers hooked up and working
in your computer, you'll also hear sounds
for various actions.

When you match all of the squares, you'll
see a big picture. You can then reset the
game or choose a different level.

TASK 36

Configuring Netscape For Helper Applications

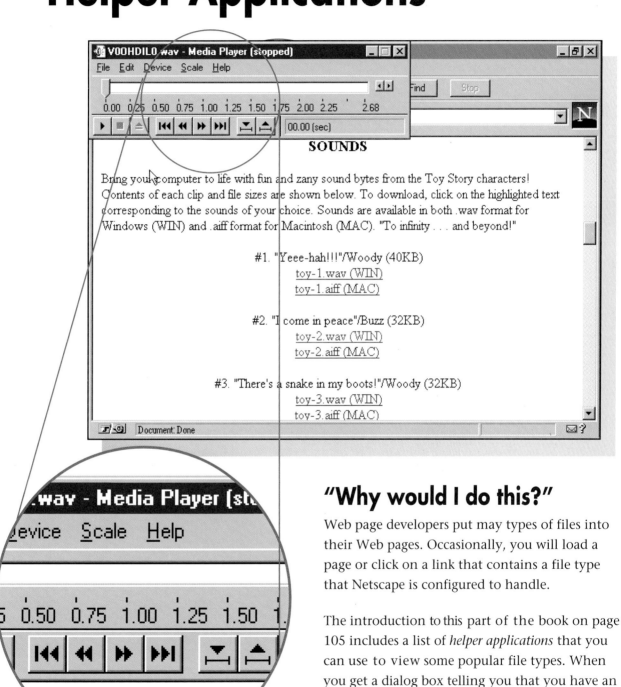

"Why would I do this?"

Web page developers put may types of files into their Web pages. Occasionally, you will load a page or click on a link that contains a file type that Netscape is configured to handle.

The introduction to this part of the book on page 105 includes a list of *helper applications* that you can use to view some popular file types. When you get a dialog box telling you that you have an unknown file type, you will need to first install the appropriate helper then follow the steps in this procedure to configure Netscape.

Task 36: Configuring Netscape For Helper Applications

1 Open the web page **http://www.toystory.com/toybox/ soundicon.htm**. Scroll down the page and find any of the links to files with a .wav extension. This task will show you how to configure Netscape to use Media Player in Windows to play these .wav files. Click on any of these .wav links.

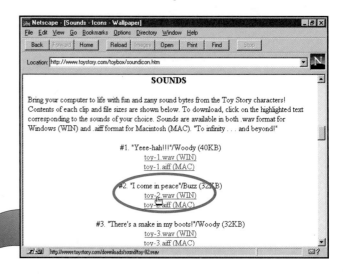

2 This opens a dialog box telling you that Netscape doesn't know what to do with this file. Since the helper we will use is Media Player and it is already installed (it is installed as part of Windows), you can clisk the **Pick App** button.

3 Click the **Browse** button.

WHY WORRY?

If you get this dialog box for a file type that you don't have an application installed for, click **Cancel** and then go get the application you need and install it before proceeding.

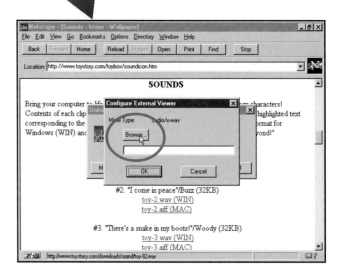

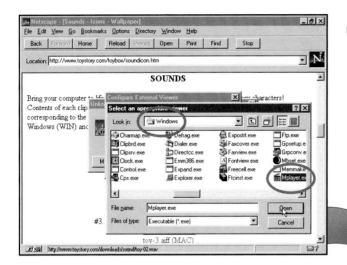

4 Change to the \Windows directory and select the Mplayer.exe file. Then click **Open**.

5 Click **OK**.

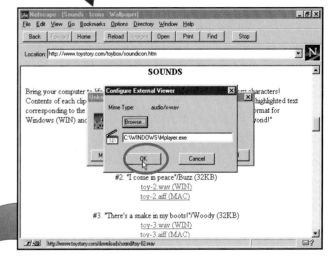

6 Netscape now begins downloading the .wav file. As it is downloaded, you will see the progress in a dialog box. This also shows the application that will be used to open it. When the file finishes downloading, the Media Player application will open (in its own window) and you will use the controls in Media Plalyer to play the sound.

Saving Movies and Sound

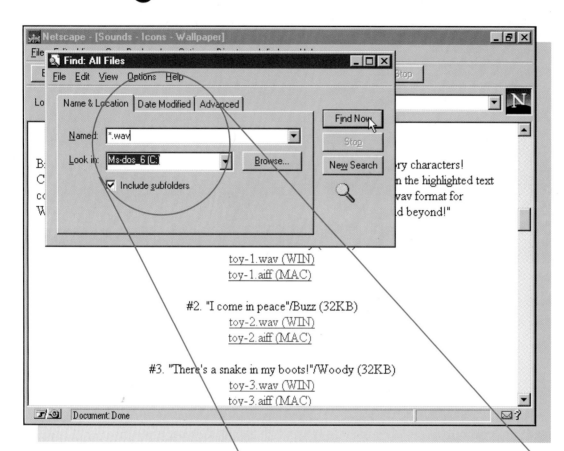

"Why would I do this?"

After you've spent 30 minutes downloading a movie, it sure would be nice to have a way to keep a copy of it so you don't have to download it again. Then you could play it again later.

This task will show you a little trick to save an audio file (or a movie file) for later use.

Be sure to do this *before* exiting Netscape. When you exit Netscape, Netscape deletes any audio or movie files you have downloaded.

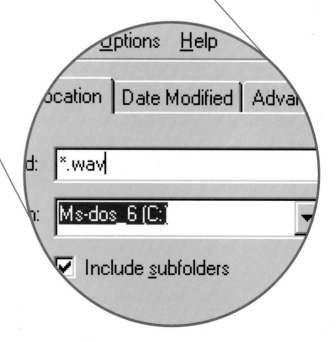

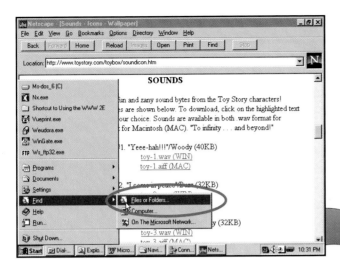

1 Open the **Start** menu and choose the **Find** option then choose the files or folders option.

2 Type ***.wav** in the Named box. Make sure Include subfolders is selected, then click **Find Now**.

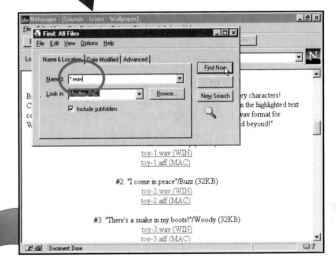

3 When the search is completed, you'll see a list of audio files. Select a file that you want to keep and then move it to another directory or change the name of the movie in this directory. If you don't do this, Netscape will delete the files from your temp directory when you exit Netscape.

PART VI

Saving, Opening, and Printing Files

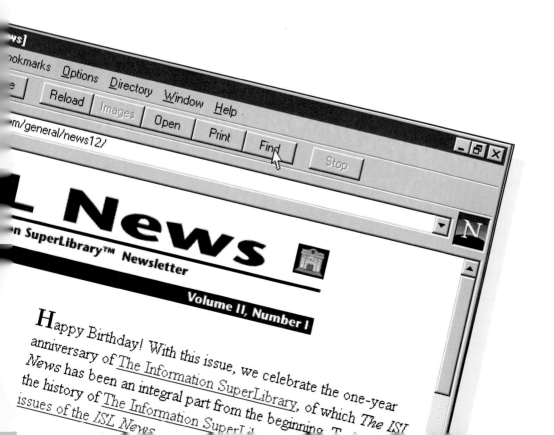

Many people spend their Web surfing time just hopping from one page to another to see what's there. If you are one of these users, you may not be all that interested in saving what you find. After all, you're just window shopping.

On the other hand, if you just spent 20 minutes searching for a Web page with the schedule for next year's NFL season, a recipe for chicken Creole, or even something for your computer like advice on configuring Windows, you will probably want to save or print what you find. Sure, you can always make a bookmark for the page and easily jump back to it whenever you want, but this may not be the most convenient way to use the document. (Especially if you are up to your elbows in chicken breasts, minced garlic, and cayenne pepper.)

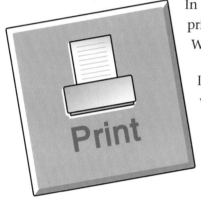

In this part, we'll look at the simple tasks of saving, opening, and printing files. If you are familiar with these tasks in any other Windows application, they will be old hat to you.

In your travels on the Web, you are sure to come across a page written by some well-intentioned but long-winded individual. You are really interested in finding what the author has to say about bandwidth on the Internet, but you can't find it for all of the filler.

This is where Netscape's find feature comes in handy. You can use this to search for and highlight text in a document. If you've used the search function in any Windows word processor or text editor, this is something that should be familiar to you and easy to learn with Netscape.

The last feature we'll take a quick look at in this part is copying text from Netscape to another Windows application. This feature is also something that is standard in Windows applications, so if you have done this elsewhere, you've got it mastered already.

The only thing different about Netscape when copying is that you can't paste text that you copy into the Netscape window. After all, what you are looking at when you view a Web page in Netscape is a file from someone else's computer. Changing the page in Netscape would require you to be able to change the file on their computer. As interactive as the Web is, that's something you won't be able to do for a while.

TASK 38

Saving and Opening Files

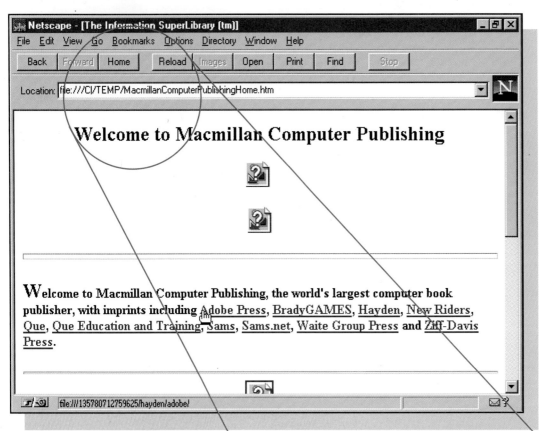

"Why would I do this?"

Being able to save files you create on a computer is one of the key functions that makes the computer useful. Otherwise, you'd have to re-create everything you want to use each time you start the computer.

Even though the files you save in Netscape aren't your own creations, it can still save you time to be able to save them and open them. We'll look at how you do that with Netscape in this task and point out a couple of common problems that you may experience.

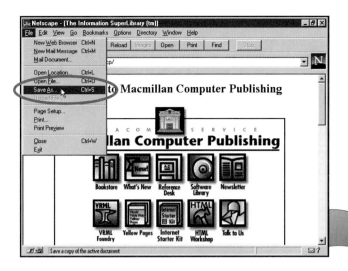

1 To see how to save pages in Netscape, open the Macmillan page at **http://www.mcp.com/mcp**. Then open the **File** menu and choose the **Save as** option.

> **NOTE** ▼
>
> The graphics on this page won't be saved; just the text is saved. When you open it, the graphics will be replaced by a missing image icon. To see how to save the graphics, see Task 31. The new Gold version of Netscape has a way to save graphics with a page.

2 Choose a directory to save the file in, and click **Save**.

> **NOTE** ▼
>
> By default, Netscape will save this file with the file name it has on the Web site you loaded it from. Some Web pages may load without a name (if the address ends in a /). For these pages, you will need to enter a file name yourself.

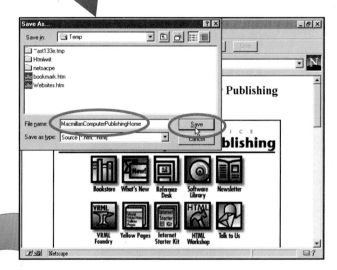

3 If you have a Web page open, and you want to save a page from one of the links instead of the page you have open, you can do that too. To see how this works, click on a link with the right mouse button. From the menu that pops up there, choose the **Save this Link as** option.

The same dialog box from step 2 will open. Choose a directory and click **OK**.

4 Once you have saved a file, you can use Netscape to open and view it again. To do this, open the **File** menu and choose the **Open File** option.

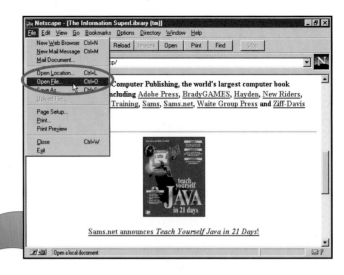

5 In the File Open dialog box, choose the correct directory and file name, and click **Open**.

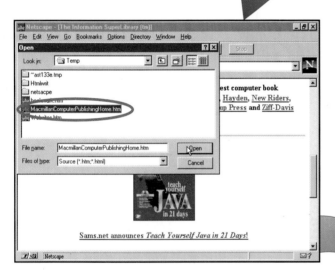

6 Move your mouse pointer so it is on the Adobe Press link and look at the address in the status bar. The address looks like it is missing something. If you wanted to load this page, you would have to start the address with **http://www.mcp.com** before what you see. What this shows you is that the Macmillan page uses a shortcut to reference other pages on this site. When you load a saved page that has this type of shortcut, you won't be able to jump to the links.

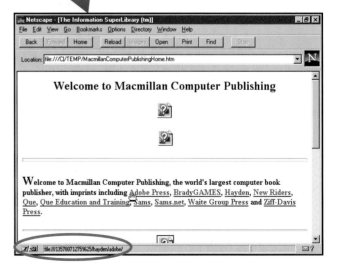

Printing a Page

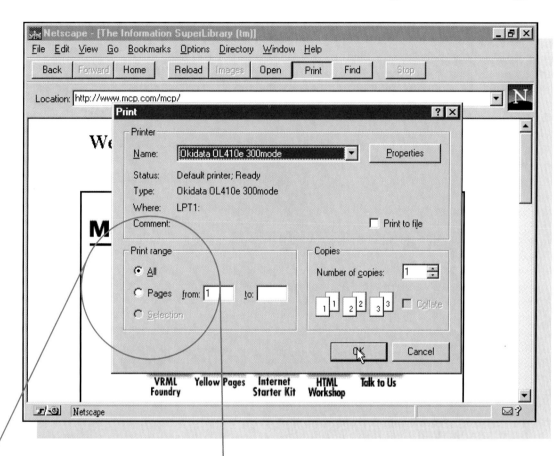

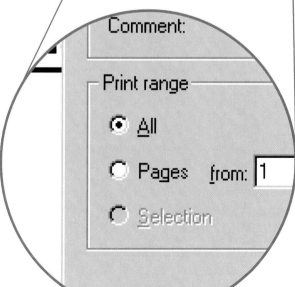

"Why would I do this?"

Netscape offers you a very simple printing procedure. When you find a Web page that you need to get a hardcopy for, printing it is straightforward.

1 From any web page click the **Print** button.

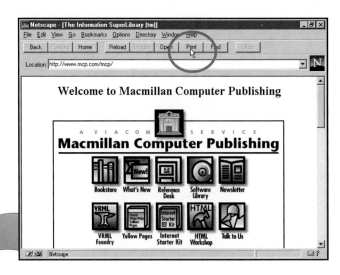

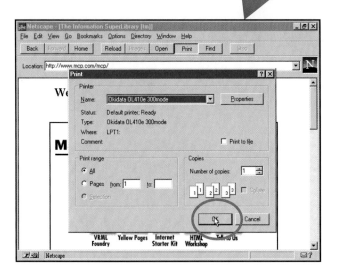

2 By default, Netscape will print one copy of the entire Web document. If you want to print more than one copy, enter the number to print in the Copies box. When are ready to print, click **OK**.

TIP ▼

You can choose different levels of quality for your printed output from the Print Quality box, if your printer supports this. Graphics take a long time to print so if you are printing just a quick and dirty copy of a page with graphics, choose a lower print quality. For high-quality graphics, choose the highest quality print available.

Searching for Text and Copying

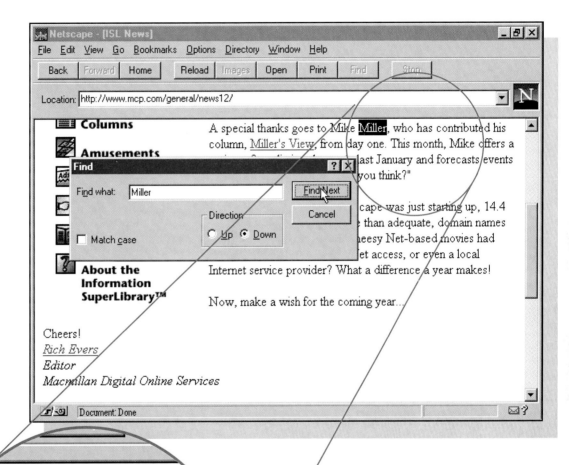

"Why would I do this?"

Just like anything else you read, sometimes you'll just want to skip to the high points in a Web page and ignore the rest. The find feature makes it easy for you to find just the parts of the page that you want to read.

And if you find something of interest that you want to copy into another document, you can do that too.

1 To search for text on a Web page, click the **Find** button.

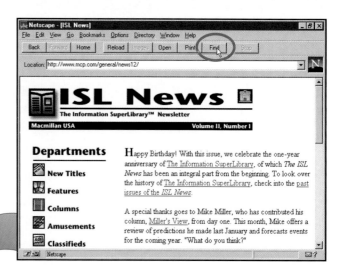

2 Enter the text you want to search for in the Find What box and then click **Find Next**.

3 Netscape will search through the document until it finds the text you entered. When it finds the text, it will be highlighted in the document. If you want to see if the text is used again, click **Find Next** again.

If the search text is not found, or after all occurrences have been found, Netscape will display a dialog box telling you that the text wasn't found. When you are done searching, click **Cancel** in the Find dialog.

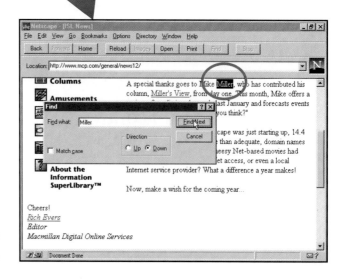

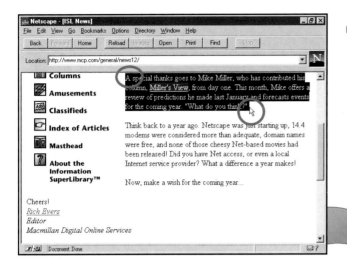

4 When you find text that you want to copy, place the mouse pointer at the beginning, click and hold the mouse button, then drag the pointer to the end of the text to select.

5 To copy the selected text so you can paste it into another document, open the **Edit** menu and choose the **Copy** option. Then, switch to that other application and follow whatever procedure you normally use to copy text into it.

WHY WORRY?

If your selection includes an image, it will not be copied or pasted into the other application. Netscape only copies the text.

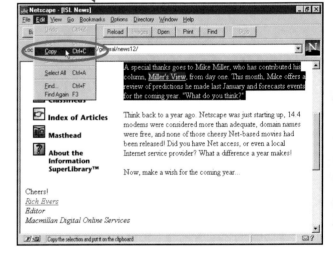

PART VII

Reading the News with Netscape

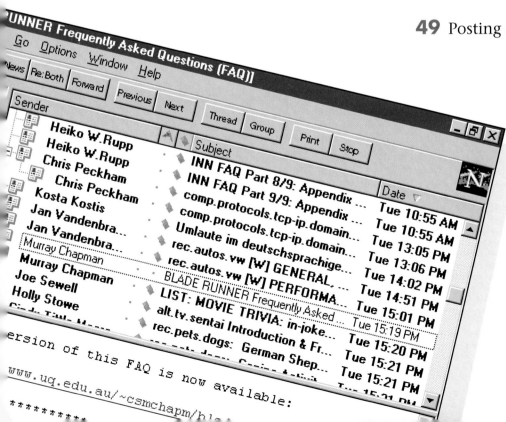

Where can you go on the Internet to discuss the failings and successes of your favorite sports team? To get advice from an expert on all of the software you use? Read movie reviews or a joke?

You can find all of this and more in UseNet newsgroups. UseNet is one of the older and more established parts of the Internet. UseNet users can post messages (called *articles*) to over 15,000 groups. Other users can then read these articles, reply to them by e-mail, or even reply with a follow-up posting.

In order to find your way around these 15,000 groups, you have to understand a little about how UseNet is organized. There are several major headings for groups (called *hierarchies*). These headings include alt, soc, rec, comp, news, and several others. These headings divide UseNet by category. The news hierarchy is about UseNet itself, soc is about social issues, comp is for computers, rec is recreation, and alt is an alternative hierarchy with fewer rules.

Within each of these hierarchies, the groups are broken down further into sub-categories. For example, in the rec group, there is a large collection of groups about sports, several about music, and so on. The sports groups break down further by type of sport. Each group has a specific name that should help you understand the type of articles you will find there. The name will look something like rec.sport.baseball.college. This would be a group in the recreational hierarchy about college baseball.

With this many newsgroups and with some of the groups having hundreds of messages a day, there is no way that you can pay attention to more than a few groups on a regular basis. The groups that you want to follow regularly, you subscribe to. When you subscribe to a group, Netscape keeps track of which articles you have read and which you haven't seen yet. This keeps you from having to sort through hundreds of articles to find the ones you haven't seen.

Another key concept to understand about news is called *threads*. When one person posts an article and then someone else responds to it with a follow-up article, the original article and reply together are called a thread. Several people can respond to the same original article, and people can respond to the responses, and respond to the responses to the responses, and so on.

An original article in a newsgroup will have a subject that looks something like this:

```
Tori Amos Concert Schedule?
```

If anyone replies, the subject would then look like this:

```
Re: Tori Amos Concert Schedule?
```

A reply to that reply would have another Re: in front of it, and so on.

This gets a little awkward, so in Netscape you will see that each level of replies is indented, which makes it easy to see who is replying to whom.

One final feature that you will really grow to like in Netscape is how it handles Internet addresses in messages. Suppose you are reading the newsgroup alt.fan.tori-amos and one of the articles there mentions the address of a great Web page all about Tori. With Netscape, you can just click on that address, and like any other link, Netscape will open the Web page. Voila!

Before you jump on to the tasks, there is one last thing you need to understand about UseNet. Every day, tens of thousands of messages are posted to UseNet. These messages can total hundreds of megabytes of files over the course of a week. Your Internet service provider probably doesn't have enough disk space to store all of the articles for a long time.

Most service providers have to delete old messages (which is called *expiring*) after a few days, or a week at most, to make room for new ones. So the articles that you see in the tasks in this book won't be on UseNet when you read the tasks. You'll still be able to use the same techniques shown in the tasks, you just won't see the same articles.

TASK 41

Telling Netscape Where to Find Your News

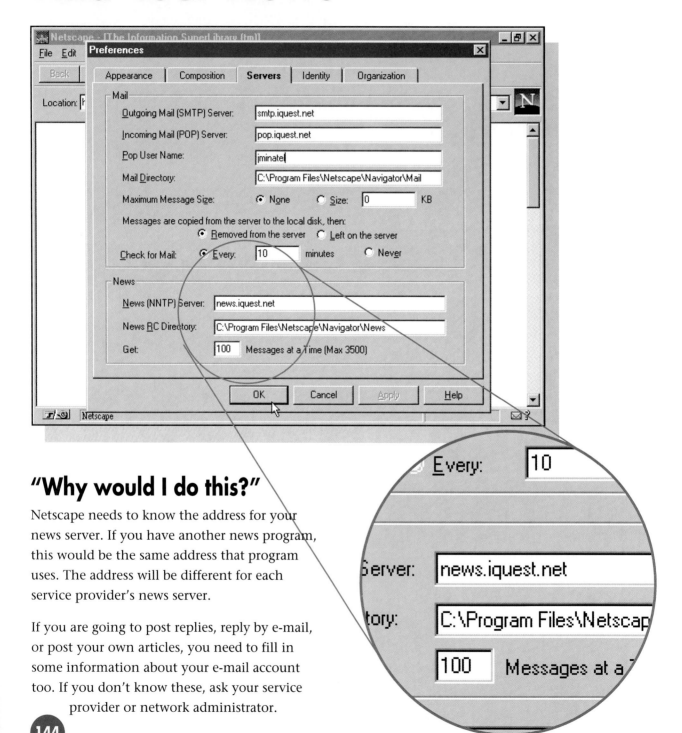

"Why would I do this?"

Netscape needs to know the address for your news server. If you have another news program, this would be the same address that program uses. The address will be different for each service provider's news server.

If you are going to post replies, reply by e-mail, or post your own articles, you need to fill in some information about your e-mail account too. If you don't know these, ask your service provider or network administrator.

144

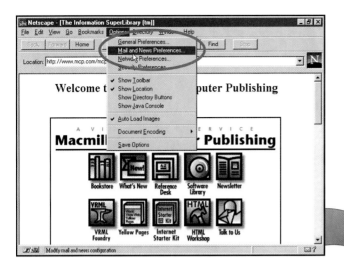

1 Open the **Options** menu and choose **Mail and News Preferences**.

NOTE ▼

We'll also set your mail preferences here, so you can use mail in tasks 51 and 52. You also need these set to post and reply to news.

2 When this dialog first opens, the value in the News [NNTP] Server box will be "news." In the Outgoing Mail (SMTP) Server you should see "mail."

In order to be able to read news, replace "news" in the News [NNTP] Server box with the address of your news server.

NOTE ▼

If you ask your service provider for the address of your mail server, specify that you need the SMTP and POP addresses.

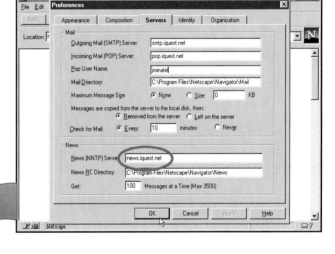

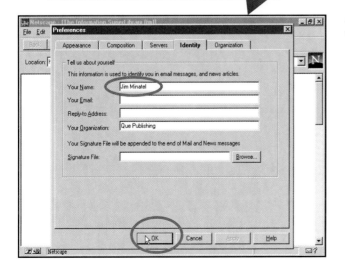

3 Enter the address of your mail servers in the Outgoing Mail (SMTP) Server and Incoming Mail (POP) Server boxes. Enter your name and complete e-mail address in the boxes. Click the **Identity** tab and enter your name and e-mail address there. When you are done, click **OK**.

Getting a List of Newsgroups

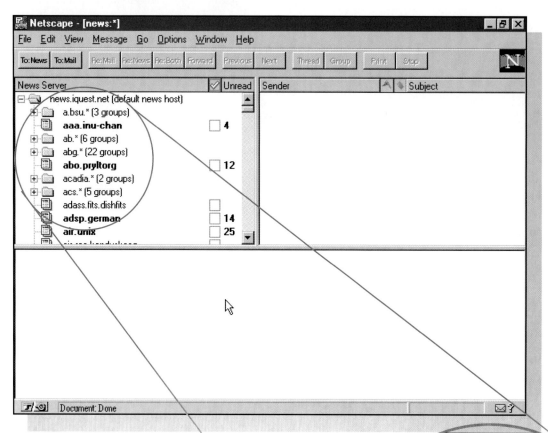

"Why would I do this?"

Once you have configured Netscape to read your news, you are ready to get a list of groups that you can read. By default, Netscape selects several groups for you that are good for new users to read.

1 Open the **Window** menu and choose the **Netscape News** option.

2 The first time that you choose this, Netscape shows you three groups that you are subscribed to automatically.

To see the rest of the groups your server carries, open the **Options** menu and choose the **Show all Newsgroups** option.

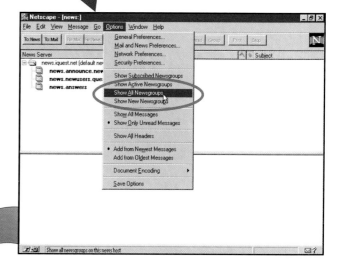

3 Netscape informs you that it will take a few minutes to retrieve the list. Click **OK**.

TASK 43

Subscribing to Newsgroups

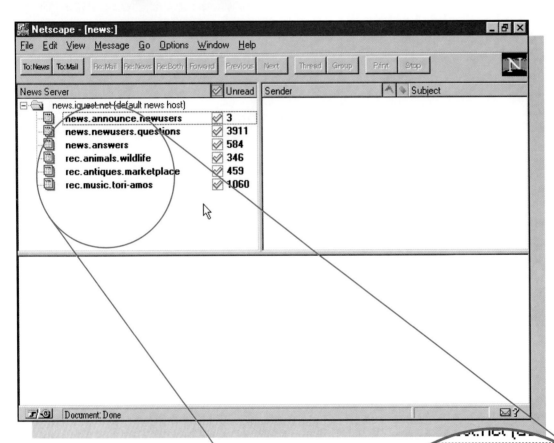

"Why would I do this?"

This task shows you how to subscribe to a group by name. You don't have to subscribe to a group to read articles in it. You can read articles without subscribing by clicking the group name in any of the lists of groups in steps 4 or 5 in this task. However, if you read articles in a group this way, the group won't be listed in your Subscribed Newsgroups page and you won't have easy access to it.

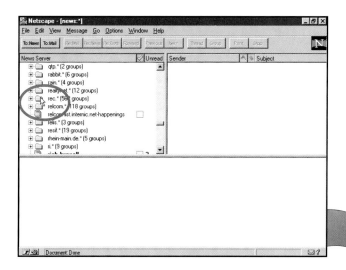

1 In the Netscape News window, scroll through the list of groups to find a group that interests you.

Groups are indicated by an icon that looks like a stack of newspapers. Categories of groups are marked with a folder icon.

To open a category, double click on it.

2 When you find a group you want to subscribe to, click the box to the right of the group name. Subscribed groups are marked with a checkmark in this box. The number to the right of the box shows the number of messages in the group that you have not read.

NOTE ▼

Some newsgroups contain content that some users find offensive. If you see a group that you find offensive, don't subscribe to it.

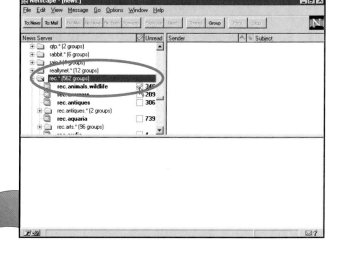

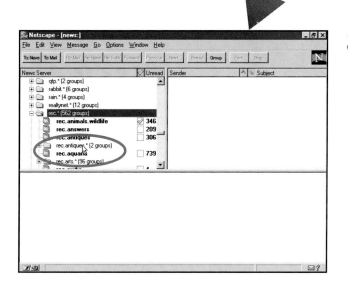

3 Catagories can contain additional sub-categories as well. As shown here, the folders indented under the rec.* category are subcategories and look for more groups by clicking their folder.

TIP ▼

Articles and lists of newsgroups can take a lot of memory to save so you may increase the cache settings if you plan to use Netscape for reading news frequently (see Task 29). You may also change the Verify Documents setting in the Cache preferences to Once per Session to speed up newsreading.

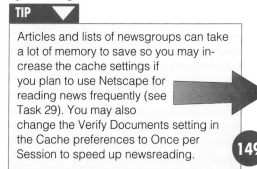

4 This tree-like structure continues through many layers of categories and groups. You can open categories or subscribe to individual groups at any of these levels in the tree.

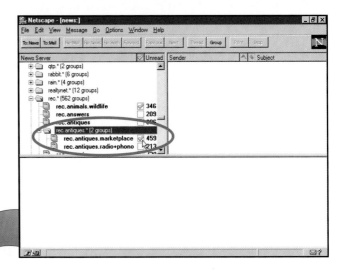

5 Once you have subscribed to some groups, it will be easier to find these groups if you hide the unsubscribed groups in the list. To do this, open the **Options** menu and choose the **Show Subscribed Newsgroups** option. (To see all of the groups again, open the nemu and choose **Show All Newsgroups**.)

6 Now the list shows just the names of the groups you are subscribed to along with the number of unread messages.

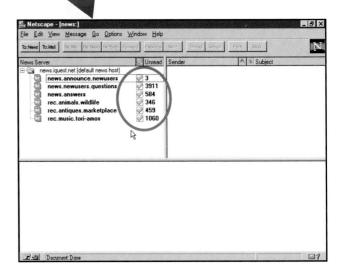

Reading Articles

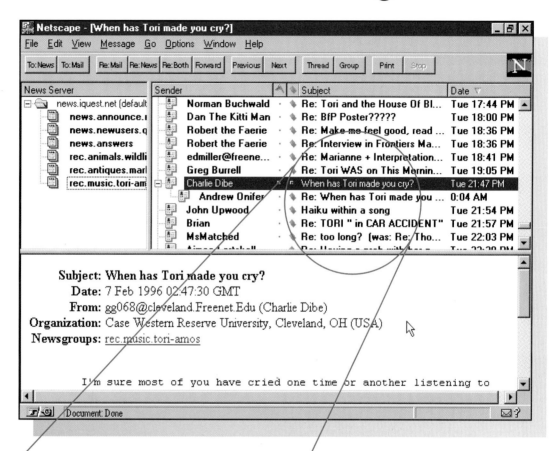

"Why would I do this?"

After you have subscribed to some groups, you are ready to read articles in any of them. As you will see in this task, reading the news is as simple as point and click.

1 In the Netscape News window, click one of the group names in your list of subscribed groups.

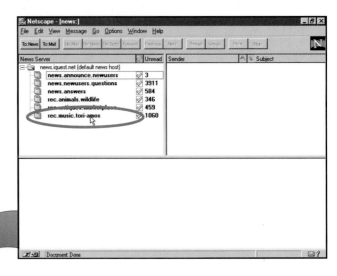

2 Now the top right part of the window contains a list of articles. Look through the group for an article that interests you. The list contains the subject and author's name for each article. The Articles that are indented are parts of threads. To read one of the articles, click it in the list.

NOTE ▼

If you don't want to remain subscribed to this group, click the box next to the group name and remove the checkmark.

3 The text of the article will open in the bottom of the window. When the article opens, you can read it, scroll through it, or print it, just like any page in Netscape.

After you have read the article, you can read any other article in the list by clicking it in the list.

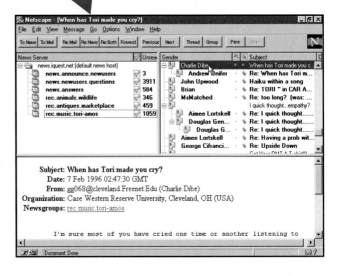

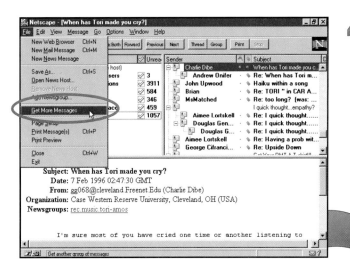

4 By default, Netscape loads 100 articles in a group at a time. If there are more than 100 articles, you will have to load the other articles to read them. To load more articles, open the **File** menu and choose the **Get More Messages** option.

5 If you have trouble seeing the group or article names in the list, you can adjust the size of the various sections of the window. To adjust the divider between the left and right side of the top of the window, put the mouse pointer over the bar between them until it changes to a double sided arrow. Then drag the bar to where you want it.

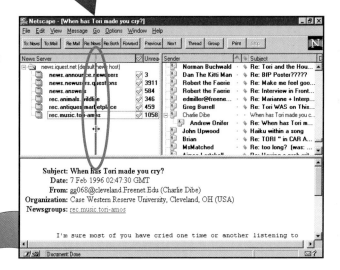

6 To adjust the size of the columns within the windows, place the mouse over the line between the column headings. The pointer will change to a double arrow. Drag the line to change the size of the columns to see more or less in that column.

Following Threads

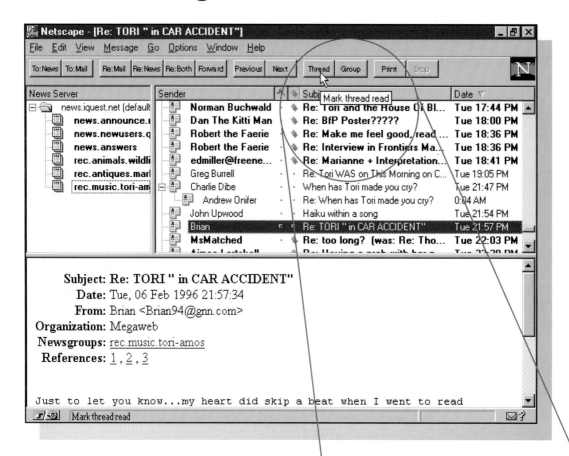

"Why would I do this?"

When someone replies to a posted article, that article and the reply are called a thread. Netscape makes it easy to read the articles in a thread in sequence, which is known as following the thread.

Some older news servers don't support the commands Netscape uses to follow threads. If your news server is like this, you will not see the indented threads and buttons described in this task.

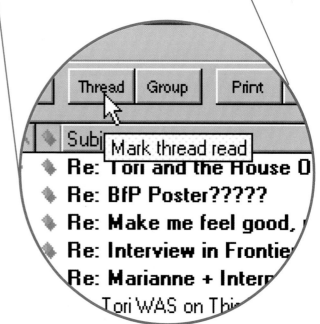

1 Open a newsgroup and look at the list of articles. Original articles are listed in a column. Replies to the article are indented.

The original article in a thread may be deleted from the server while replies are still coming in. The subject of a thread like this will still be listed in the second column, but there won't be an author name.

2 When you read an article that is part of a thread, click the next button to jump to the next article in the thread. To jump to previous articles in the thread, click the previous button.

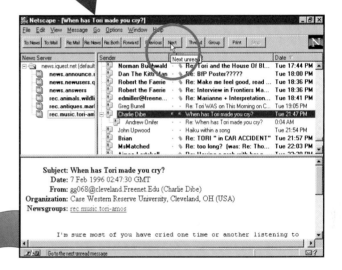

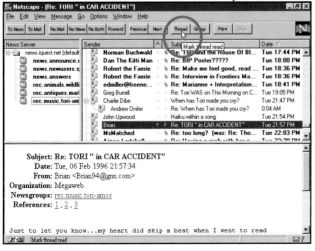

3 To mark all of the articles that are part of the current thread as having been read, click on the **Catch Up Thread** button.

> **NOTE** ▼
>
> Articles that are a reply to another article are automatically named with the same subject preceded by Re: You can mark all of the articles in a group read by clicking the Group button.

Jumping to Cross Posts and Links

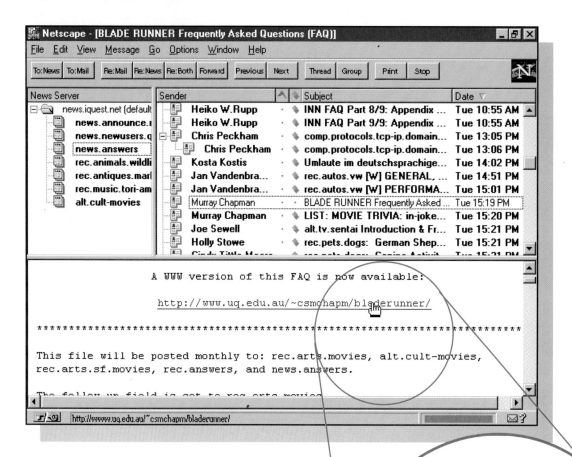

"Why would I do this?"

When a person posts the same article to more than one group at once, the article has been crossposted. If you read a crossposted article, you may want to jump to one of the other groups it is posted in to see if there are other articles of interest.

Netscape helps you use Internet addresses that are mentioned in news articles. If someone includes the address of a Web page in an article, Netscape makes it a link that you can click.

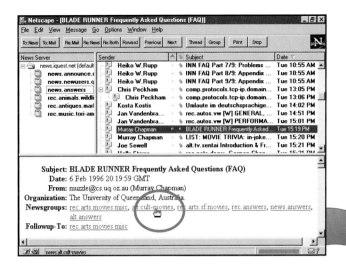

1 When an article has been crossposted, you will see more than one group name listed on the Newsgroups line in the article. To jump to the list of articles in one of the other groups listed, click its name. Here, I am clicking the **alt.cult-movies** link to jump to that group.

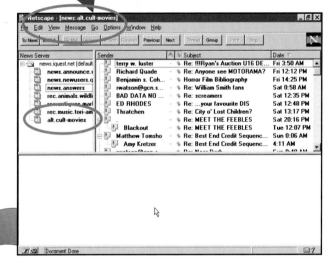

2 This will open the list of articles in the alt.answers group as shown here. This does not subscribe you to this group, though. If you want to subscribe, you will have to check the box in the group list.

3 When you find a news article that mentions a Web page you want to see, all you need to do is click the page's address in the article. If the author of the article typed the address correctly, Netscape will open the listed Web page.

Posting a Follow-up Article

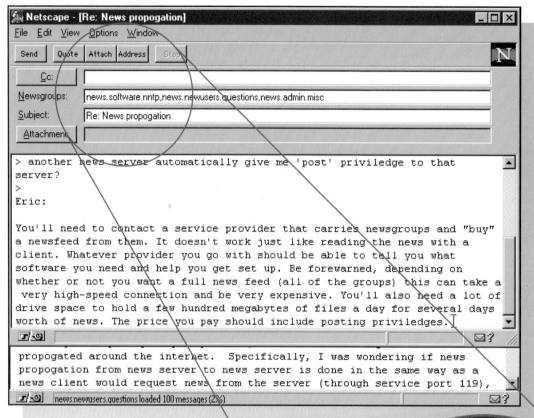

"Why would I do this?"

With a newspaper, if you see a story you would like to respond to, you can write a letter to the editor to give your opinion. But that's not very convenient, and there is no guarantee your reply will ever be seen.

With UseNet, you can read an article and reply (called posting a follow-up) all in the same place. Everyone who reads the original article can see your follow-up article. UseNet is a true interactive news system.

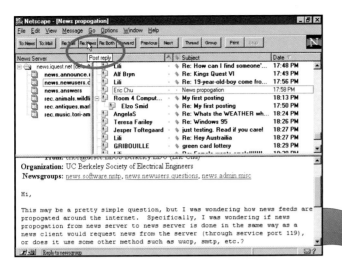

1 When you find an article you want to post a follow-up to, click the **Re:News** button.

2 When you click the re:News button, a window to create your reply will open. Netscape will automatically fill in the article subject and the name of the group. (If the original article was cross-posted there will be more than one group in the Newsgroups box.)

Type the body of your reply in the dialog box. The original post will be quoted with > characters to the left.

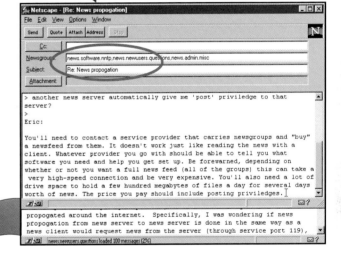

3 Quoting part of the original article is a good idea so that people reading your follow-up know what you are replying to. Don't include the entire original article though. Delete everything that doesn't directly relate to your reply. This saves readers from having to sort through too much text that they saw in the original article.

When you are ready to post the follow-up, click the **Send** button.

Replying by E-mail

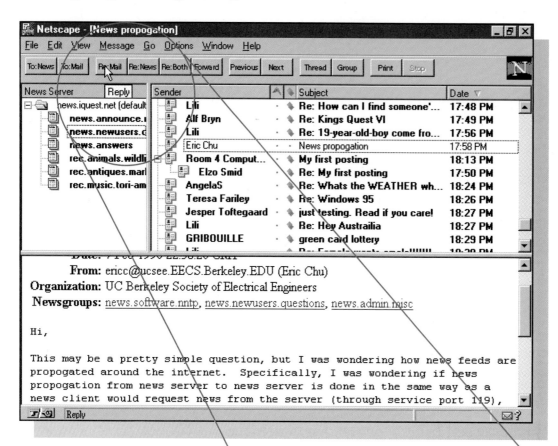

"Why would I do this?"

In addition to posting a follow-up to a newsgroup so that everyone can read it, you can also send a reply to the original poster.

Sometimes it is best to reply to the sender. If your reply is not likely to be of interest to others in the group or needs to be private, send it by e-mail rather than posting a follow-up.

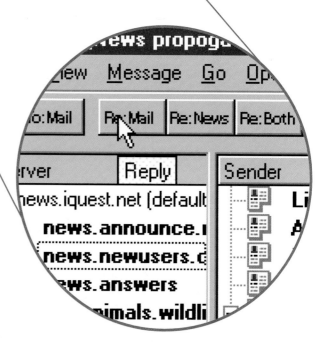

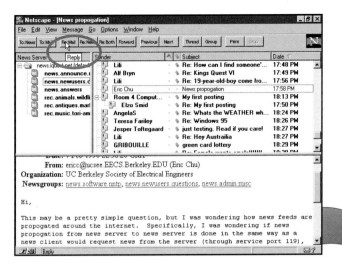

1 When you find an article you want to reply to by e-mail, click the **Re:Mail** button.

WHY WORRY?

If you didn't enter your e-mail address and an address for your e-mail server in the Preferences dialog box in Task 41, you will not be able to send mail or post replies.

2 The same dialog box you would use to post a follow-up opens. This time, a Mail To box, and the Subject are filled in.

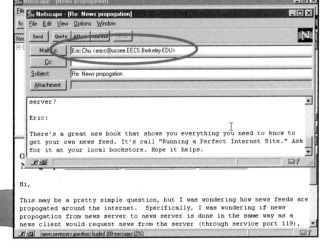

3 Type the text of your reply in the dialog box. Text from the original article is included as in the previous task. When you are ready to send the reply, click the **Send** button.

Posting a New Article

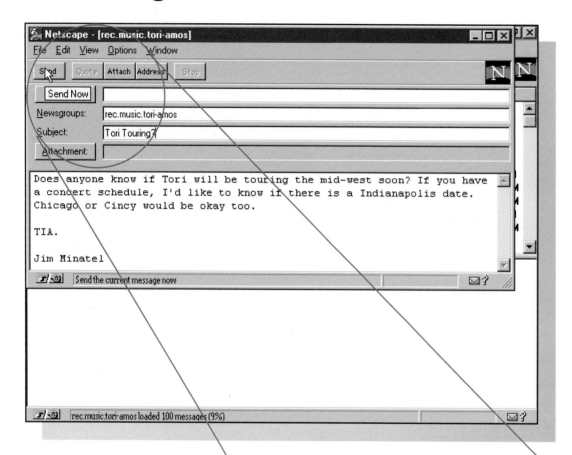

"Why would I do this?"

After you have read other people's posts for a few days (or a few weeks) you may be ready to post an article yourself. Before you do, keep these few things in mind. First, in most groups, only a small percentage of users ever post an article. Most people subscribing to the group just read (called *lurking*), which is perfectly acceptable in most groups. Most groups frown on posts for the sake of posting. Second, be sure the subject of your post is appropriate for the group. Finally, be considerate of others in the content of your posts.

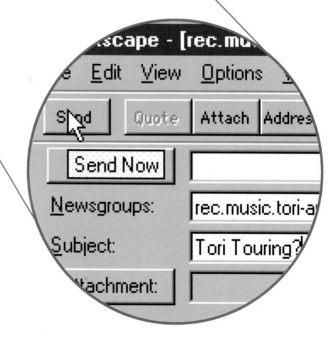

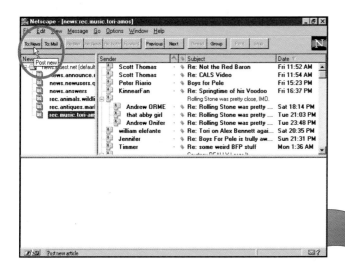

1 To post an original article to a group, select that group in the list. Click the **To:News** button.

2 The same dialog box that you used to post a follow-up or send a mail reply opens. The name of the group will be filled in for you in the Newsgroups box.

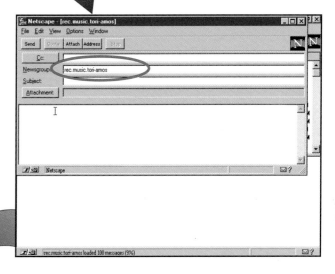

3 Enter a subject for your post in the Subject box. Try to keep the subject descriptive and concise.

Enter the body of your message in the dialog box. When you are done, click the **Send** button.

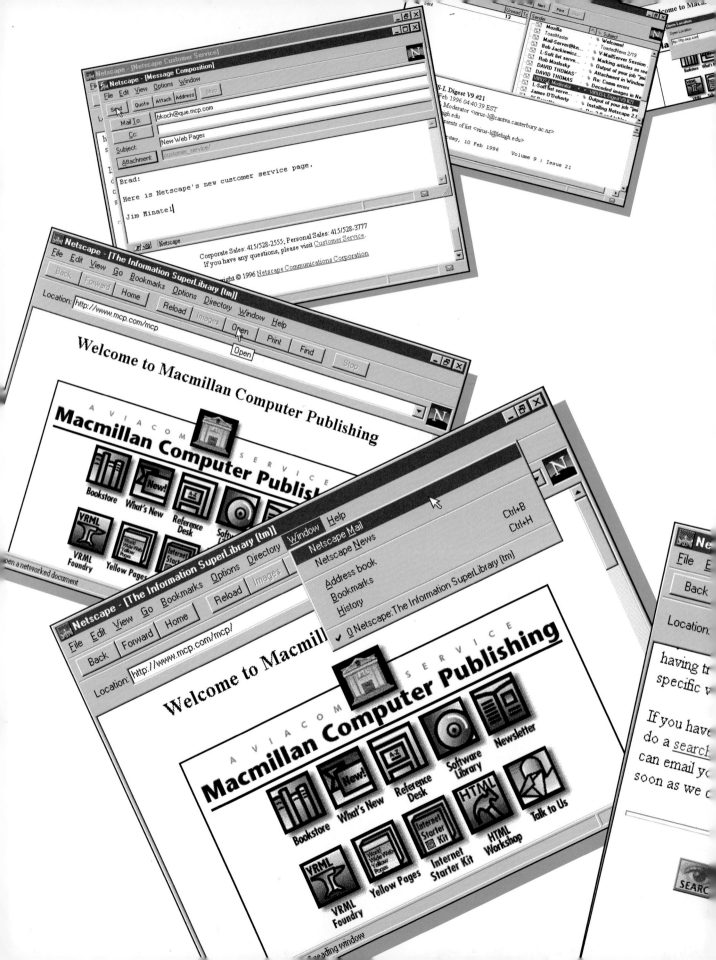

PART VIII
FTP and E-mail

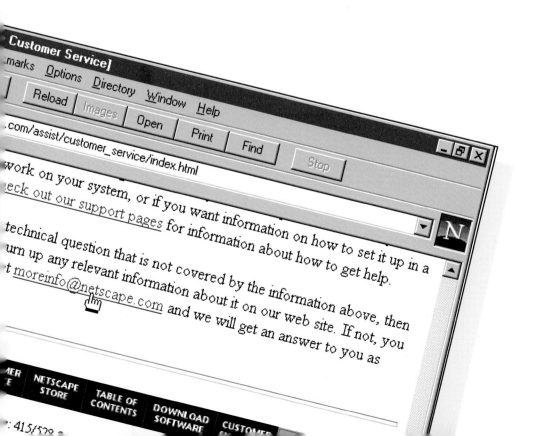

As you saw in Part VII of this book, Netscape is more than just a Web browser. In that part, you found out how to read UseNet news with Netscape. In this part, we'll look at Netscape's capabilities to get files by FTP and transfer e-mail.

FTP (short for *file transfer protocol*) is one of the oldest parts of the Internet. But just because it's old, don't write it off as over the hill. It is still one of the most used services on the Internet.

FTP is a system for sending files across the Internet. FTP sites are computers with files that users can access and copy to their own computers. Many of these sites use a courtesy system known as *anonymous FTP* to allow any user to log on to their site and copy files. Netscape can be used to access anonymous FTP sites and transfer files. Unlike the Web, FTP sites are not connected together. You have to access each one individually.

There are two ways you can access FTP sites from Netscape. First, Web pages can have built-in links to FTP sites. In fact, you have already seen this type of link in Task 33. When you retrieved the files for Shockwave, you were connecting to FTP sites from links on Web pages.

The other way is to access the site by entering its address in Netscape's Location bar or Open box. When you use Netscape to access an FTP site this way, you add ftp:// to the beginning of the address. So if the address for the site is ftp.mcp.com, you would type **ftp://ftp.mcp.com**.

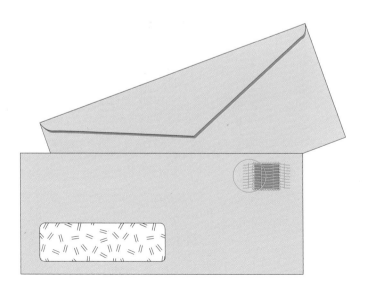

The last part of the Internet that we will look at in this part is e-mail. Netscape has added a powerful e-mail component to the program with this latest release. You can now handle all of your e-mail needs within Netscape. (There are still a few advanced capabilities in programs like Eudora Pro that you won't find in Netscape but most users will find that Netscape has all of the features they need for e-mail.)

Like FTP and Gopher, there are two ways to send e-mail with Netscape. First, many people who create Web pages include their e-mail addresses as links. Many companies that use the Web for customer support also include links to their addresses to make it easy to send mail. Netscape makes it easy to send mail to these links by opening the mail dialog box when you click on the link.

Netscape also has the ability to read your incoming e-mail. If you read the tasks in the previous part of the book dealing with UseNet, you'll find that Netscape's e-mail reader is very similar to the New Window, and learning one after you know the other is simple.

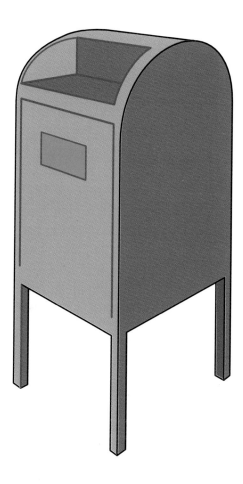

Getting Files by FTP

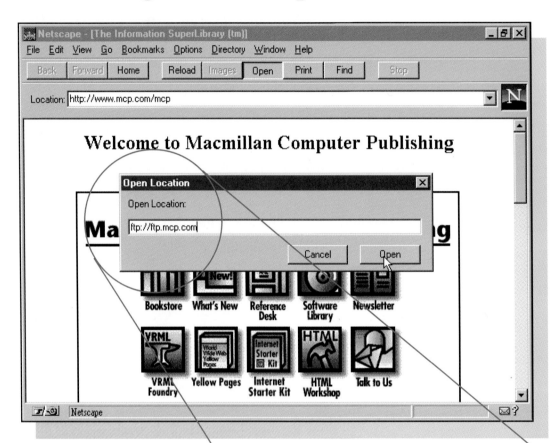

"Why would I do this?"

FTP makes a huge system of files available to you. You can connect to thousands of FTP servers. These servers have hundreds of gigabytes of files such as shareware and freeware software, text files, graphics, and more available for you to download.

Because the Internet also includes UNIX, Macs, and other types of computers, you will find some files on FTP sites that you can't use. Many graphics and text files can be viewed in Windows regardless of the type of computer that created them.

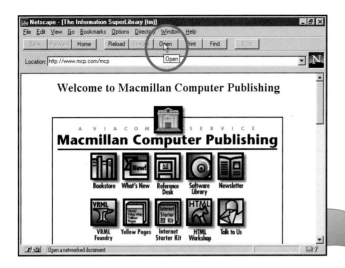

1 To open an FTP site that you have the address for, click the **Open** button.

NOTE ▼

If you see a link to an FTP site in a Web page, just click on it and it will open like any other page in Netscape.

2 Enter the address for the FTP site in the Open Location dialog box. To follow along, enter **ftp://ftp.mcp.com** and then click **Open**.

WHY WORRY?

FTP sites have to limit the number of people who can connect at once. If you get an error message and Netscape can't connect, this is usually the cause. If this happens, just try again at a different time.

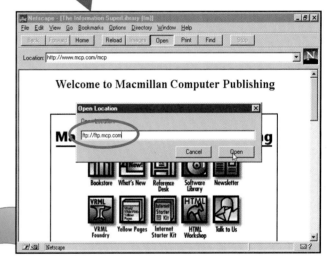

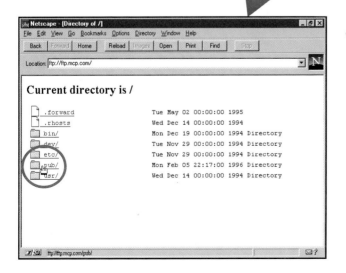

3 When the FTP site opens, you will see a list of all the directories there. If there is a pub or public directory, this is a good place to start looking. Click the **pub** folder to see the subdirectories.

4 To continue following along here, click the **software** folder.

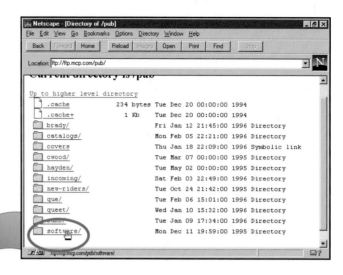

5 If you see something of interest to you here, click on it. To follow this task, click **games**.

NOTE ▼

Notice that the Location bar contains the complete address for the site and the path to the directory that you are in. If you know the directory you want to go to, you can enter the address and directory in this style in step 2.

6 In the games directory, you will see a long list of files, the file size, and other information about the files. Scroll through the list until you see the text file **doommd.txt**. Netscape can display text files for you to read. Click on this file.

NOTE ▼

If you don't know where to find what you need at an FTP site, look for a file with a name like index.txt or files.txt. This file should list the files and directories at the site.

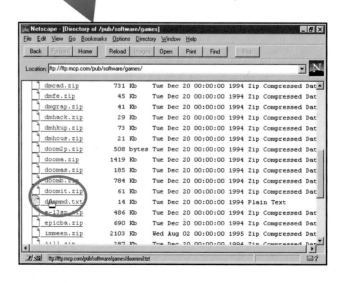

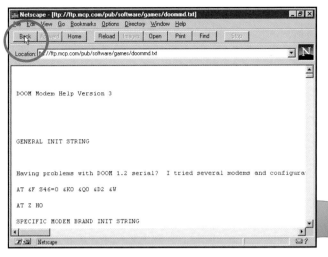

7 The text file is now displayed in Netscape. To go back to the directory listing, click the **Back** button.

> **NOTE** ▼
>
> You can save one of these text files just like any other file in Netscape by opening the **File** menu and choosing the **Save as** option. If you are going to download a large text file, you may want to save it first and view it in another program instead of Netscape. To do this, click the filename with the right mouse button and choose the **Save this link as** option.

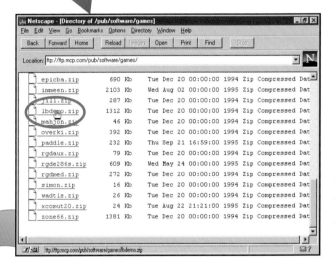

8 To download any other kind of file, just click on it. If it is a GIF, JPEG, or another kind of file that you have a viewer installed and configured for, Netscape will display it.

The file we are clicking here, **lbdemo.zip**, contains an extra level for the popular game DOOM.

9 If it isn't a file that Netscape can display or start a viewer for, you'll see an Unknown File Type dialog box. Click the **Save File** button. After that, pick a location to save it in the dialog box and click **Save**.

> **NOTE** ▼
>
> Most files at FTP sites are zipped and will need to be unzipped to use. If you don't have WinZip or another program for unzipping files, see the introduction to Part V for where to get it.

Reading E-mail

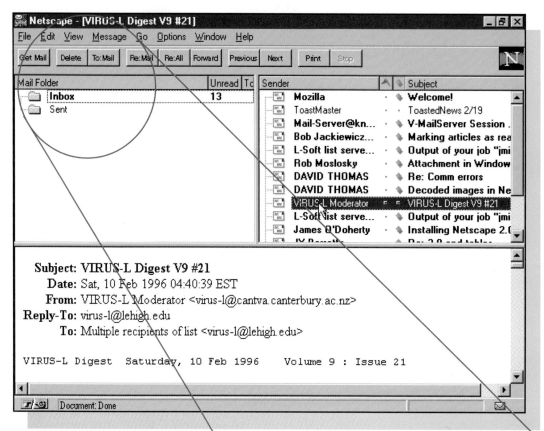

"Why would I do this?"

E-mail is one of the oldest uses of the internet. And as popular as the Web is, more people use e-mail than the Web. With that in mind, almost everyone who uses the Internet will want to know how to read the e-mail that other people send to them.

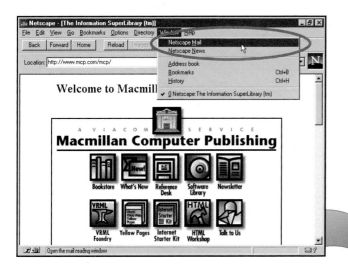

1 To open the Netscape mail window, open the **Window** menu and choose the **Netscape Mail** option.

WHY WORRY?

Be sure that you entered all of your e-mail identification information in task 41 or you won't be able to receive or send e-mail.

2 This opens the Netscape mail window. The top left pane shows your Inbox. The one message that is there by default is a welcome message that is included with Netscape by the installation program. To get any real mail you have, click the **Get Mail** button.

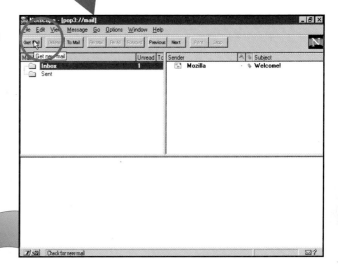

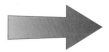

3 This prompts you for your e-mail password. Enter the password and click **OK**.

4 Netscape will retrieve your e-mail. The number of messages unread in your inbox will be updated. The upper right part of the screen will show a list of e-mail that you have waiting to be read. The list shows the sender and the subject. To read a message, click on it in the list. This opens the text of the message in the bottom part of the window.

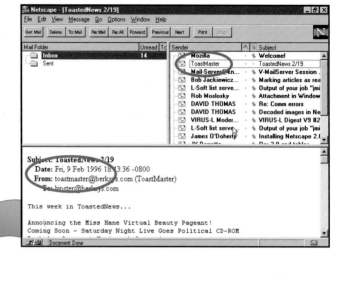

5 The bottom window shows not just the text of the message but also the complete name and e-mail address of the sender, the subject, the date it was sent, and other information about the message.

TIP ▼

You can also rearrange the size of the various parts of the Mail window and columns, using the same click and drag techniques that were shown for the news window in steps 5 and 6 of task 44.

6 If a web page address (or other URL) is included as part of a mail message, you can click the address to open that page in Netscape.

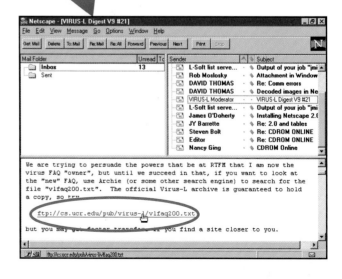

Sending E-mail

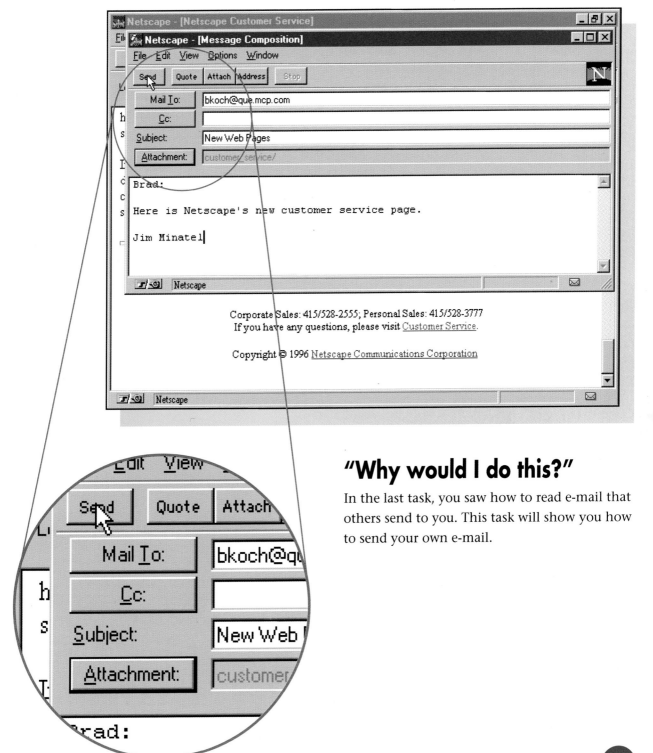

"Why would I do this?"

In the last task, you saw how to read e-mail that others send to you. This task will show you how to send your own e-mail.

1 One way to send e-mail from Netscape is to click on an e-mail address link in a web page. An example of one of these can be found in the page at http://home.netscape.com/assist/customer_service/index.html. If you click the e-mail link in that page, it will open the mail composition window (like the one shown in step 3 here) and fill in the address for you.

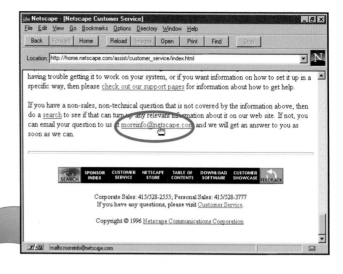

2 The other way to open the Netscape mail composition window dowsn't depend on finding a web page with an address. To do this, open the File menu and choose the **New Mail Message** option.

WHY WORRY?

Be sure that you entered all of your e-mail identification information in task 41 or you won't be able to receive or send e-mail.

3 The Message Composition dialog box will open. To send mail enter a subject and the address of the recipient in the Mail To box. You can also attach a copy of the current web page. To do this, click the **Attachment** button.

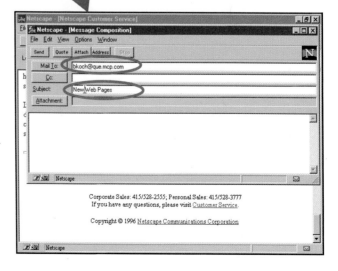

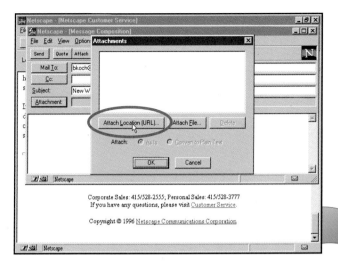

4 If you click the **Attachment** button, Netscape will open the Attachments dialog box. Click the **Attach Location (URL)** button.

5 The address of the current web page will be entered. Accept this and click **OK** or enter another address.

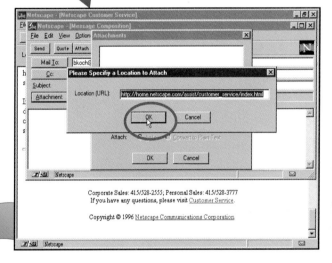

6 The Attachments dialog box will be filled in with the address of the page. Click **OK**.

This takes you back to the message composition dialog box. Enter the text of your message there and click **Send**.

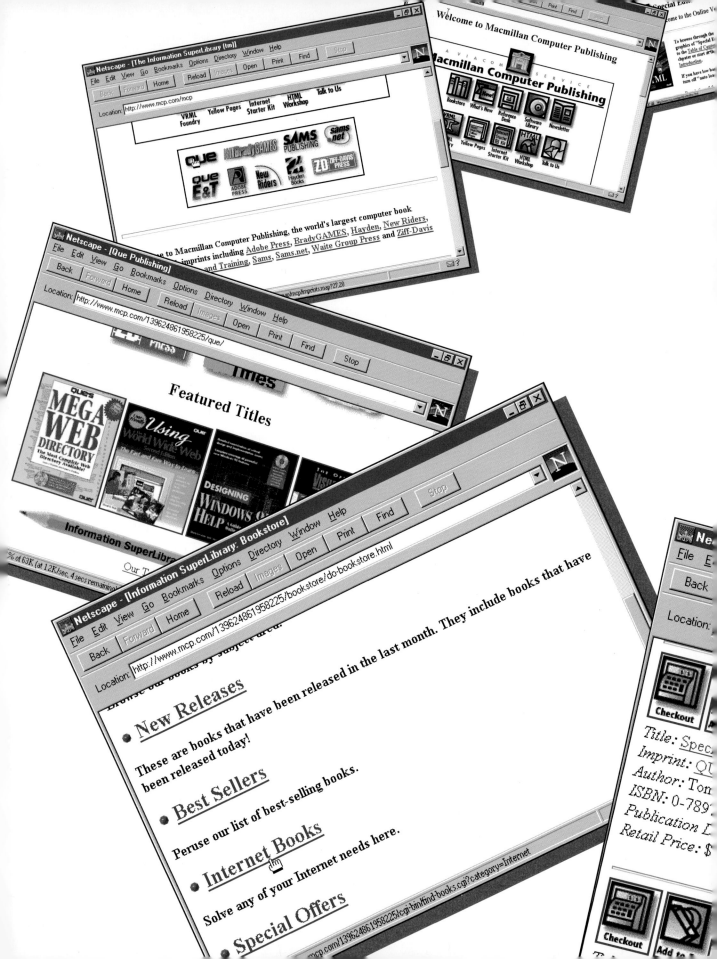

PART IX

What's Hot on the Web

53 The Macmillan Information SuperLibrary

54 Hot Web Sites

In this last part, we are going to take a quick look at the Web site from Macmillan Computer Publishing. Macmillan is the parent company for Que, this book's publisher.

The other task in this part is a list of some Web sites you may want to explore. It includes brief descriptions and addresses.

The Macmillan Information SuperLibrary

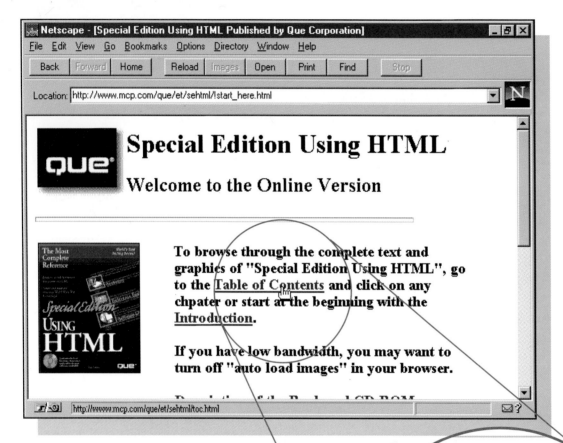

"Why would I do this?"

Macmillan has assembled a large Web site with a wealth of information about computers and Macmillan's books. In this task, you will see how you can find a book about a particular topic. Some books here have special features like an online version you can browse before buying.

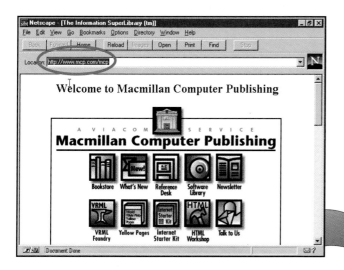

1 Click the **Open** button and enter the address **http://www.mcp.com/mcp**, then click **Open**. This opens the page shown here.

2 To see information about any of the publishers that are part of Macmillan (including Que), scroll down the page and click the link for that publisher.

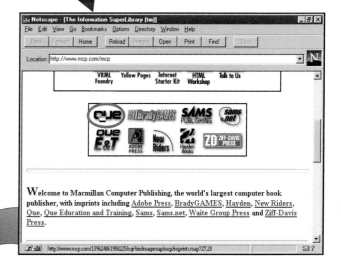

3 The page for Que tells you a little about Que and the three main areas that Que concentrates its publishing efforts on. To see more about any one of these you can click it.

At the bottom of each page, there are links to the other parts of the Macmillan Web site. Click the **Bookstore** link to find out information about books that are available from Macmillan.

4 This opens a list of links to books by category. There are also links for New Releases, Special Offers (for online customers only), and to a list of all titles. Here, click the **Internet Books** link.

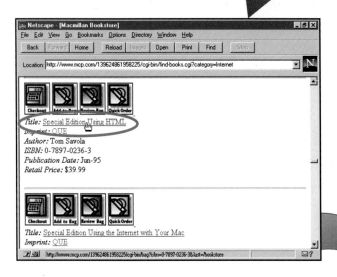

5 Information about the books, including the author's name, when it was published, and price, is given along with the title. Scroll through the list and click the **Special Edition Using HTML** link.

6 This opens a page with more detailed information about the book. You can read a brief description of the book here.

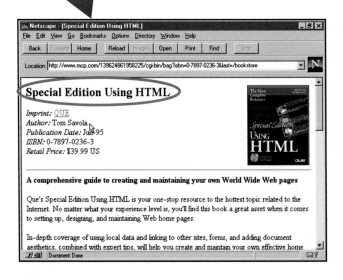

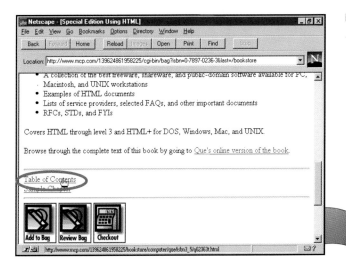

7 Scroll to the bottom of this page. There you will find links to the Table of Contents for the book and a sample chapter. To see the contents of the book, click the **Table of Contents** link.

8 This page lists the contents by chapter for the book. You can see the sample chapter by clicking the chapter that is a link.

To go back to the listing for the book, click the **Back** button.

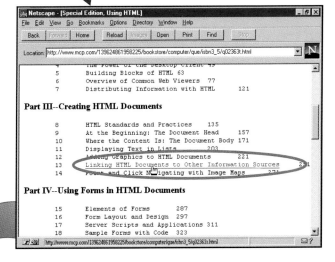

9 After you have looked at this, click the **Back** button twice.

10

Now you should be back at the page in the bookstore for *Special Edition Using HTML*. Near the bottom of this page, click the **Que's online version of the book** link.

TIP ▼

The URL for this online version is **http://www.mcp.com/et/sehtml/!start _here.html**.

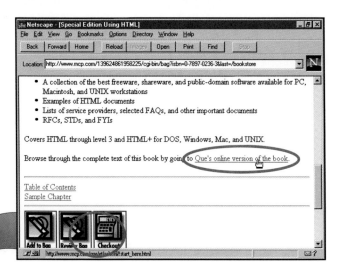

11

To see the complete table of contents for this online version, click the **Table of Contents** link.

NOTE ▼

Not all of the books in the store have online versions. This is a special feature that you will find with a few books. Other books may have links to author's home pages, updates, links to software, or other special features.

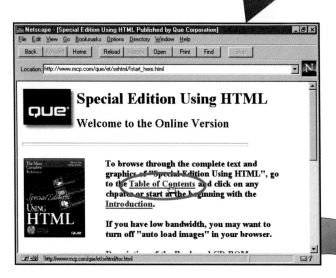

12

Click on any chapter in the table of contents to see the chapter.

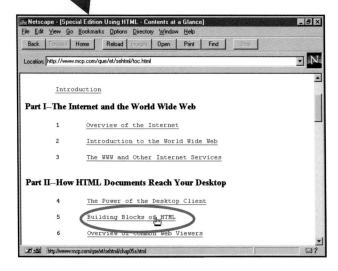

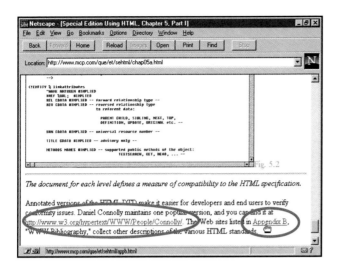

13 A portion of the chapter will load. (The chapters are broken into many small parts to keep downloads fast.) The chapter will include figures, notes, tips, captions, and everything else from the printed book.

The online version also has links from the text to any Web pages mentioned in the book. You will also find that cross-references from one part of the book to another are linked to make the book easier to navigate.

Hot Web Sites

Site Description	URL Address
1996 Olympics	http://www.atlanta.olympic.org/
Amazon Bookstore	http://www.amazon.com
Amnesty International	http://www.amnesty.org
Australian National Botanic Gardens	http://155.187.10.12/index.html
Bible Gateway	http://www.gospelcom.net/bible
Car Showroom	http://www.dealernet.com/
Career Magazine	http://www.careermag.com
CBS	http://www.cbs.com
CIA	http://www.odci.gov
CNN News	http:www.cnn.com/
Comet Shoemaker-Levy Home Page (JPL)	http://newproducts.jpl.nasa.gov/sl9/sl9.html
CommerceNet	http://www.commerce.net
Company Corporation	http://incorporate.com/tcc/home.html
Computer Professionals for Social Responsibility	http://cpsr.org/home
Confession Booth	http://anther.learning.cs.cmu.edu/priest.html
Cyberspace Report	http://www.ics.uci.edu/~ejw/csr/cyber.html
DeweyWeb	http://ics.soe.umich.edu
Dilbert	http://www.unitedmedia.com/comics/dilbert/
Dinosaurs—Honolulu Community College	http://www.hcc.hawaii.edu/dinos/dinos.1.html
Doctor Fun	http://www.unitedmedia.com/comics/drfun/
DOS and Windows Software— OAK Software Repository	http://mars.acs.oakland.edu/oak
Electronic Frontier Foundation	http://www.eff.org

Site Description	URL Address
Employment Network	http://www.espan.com/
Entertainment Weekly	http://www.timeinc.com/ew/Welcome.html
ESPN	http://espnet.sportszone.com
Federal Express	http://www.fedex.com
FedWorld	http://www.fedworld.gov
Frog Dissection	http://curry.edschool.Virginia.EDU/90/frog/
Games	http://www.gamesdomain.co.uk
Gateway 2000	http://www.gw2k.com
Golf Links	http://www.golf.com/links
HealthNet	http://debra.dgbt.doc.ca:80/~mike/healthnet
Hot Hot Hot!	http://www.hot.presence.com
HTML	http://www.mcp.com/que/et/sehtml/!start_here.html
IBM PCs	http://www.pc.ibm.com/
Indiana Hoosiers Basketball	http://www.starnews.com/ingame/iudir.html
Indiana University	http://www.indiana.edu
Internet Information	ftp://rtfm.mit.edu/pub/
Internet Shopping Network	http://shop.internet.net
Internet World Magazine	http://www.mecklerweb.com
InterNIC Home Page	http://www.internic.net
Jerusalem Mosaic	http://www1.huji.ac.il/jeru/jerusalem.html
Legal Information Institute	http://www.law.cornell.edu/lii.table.html
Legislative Information on the Internet	http://thomas.loc.gov
Library of Congress	http://lcweb.loc.gov/homepage/lchp.html
Macmillan Information SuperLibrary	http://www.mcp.com/mcp
Major League Baseball	http://www.majorleaguebaseball.com
Microsoft	http://www.microsoft.com

(continues)

Site Description	URL Address
Movie Database	http://www.msstate.edu/Movies
NASA	http://hypatia.gsfc.nasa.gov/NASA_homepage.html
Nasdaq Financial Executive Journal	http://www.law.cornell.edu/nasdaq/nasdtoc.html
Netscape	http://home.netscape.com
Novell Inc. World Wide Web Homepage	http://www.novell.com
Online Book Initiative	ftp://obi.std.com/obi
Project Gutenberg	http://jg.cso.uiuc.edu/pg_home.html
Racing Archive	http://student-www.eng.hawaii.edu/carina/ra.home.page.html
Rhino Records	http://cybertimes.com/Rhino/welcome.html
Rolling Stones	http://www.stones.com/
Shareware	http://www.shareware.com
Shopping Downtown Anywhere	http://awa.com
Sports Illustrated	http://www.timeinc.com/si
Stanford University Medical Center	http://med-www.Stanford.EDU/MedCenter/welcome-info.html
Star Trek: Voyager	http://voyager.paramount.com/
Taoism	http://www.ccs.neu.edu/home/thigpen/html/tao.html
Tarot Server	http://www.facade.com/Occult/tarot
Teacher Education Internet Server	http://curry.edschool.Virginia.EDU/insite
The Vatican	http://catholic.net/RCC/Indices/subs/vatican.html
TVNet	http://tvnet.com/
U.S. Department of Health and Human Services	http://www.os.dhhs.gov
U.S. House of Representatives	http://www.house.gov
USA Today	http://www.usatoday.com
White House	http://www.whitehouse.gov
Win 95 Magazine	http://www.win95mag.com
Windows 95 Internet Headquarters	http://www.windows95.com

Site Description	URL Address
Windows Software-Winsite	http://www.winsite.com
WWW What's New	http://www.ncsa.uiuc.edu/SDG/Software /Mosaic/Docs/whats-new.html
Zen	http://sunsite.unc.edu/zen/

Index

Symbols